THE AUF WIEDERSEHEN, PET STORY

THAT'S LIVING ALRIGHT

FRANC RODDAM AND DAN WADDELL

The authors would like to thank, in no particular order, Dick Clement, Ian La Frenais, Chris Fairbank, Tim Healy, Kevin Whately, Pat Roach, Julia Tobin, Noel Clarke, Roger Bamford, Stan Hey and John Harwood Bee for giving up their time to be interviewed. Sadly, Timothy Spall was unavailable due to filming commitments on the other side of the world. Paul Armstrong is the world's authority on *Aufpet*, and was kind enough to answer several queries and provide us with many lines of inquiry. Go visit his website at www.aufpet.com. The staff at the British Film Institute's library in London also proved invaluable in helping search for press cuttings and viewing figures. We would also like to thank everyone at BBC Books, in particular Ben Dunn and the book's editors, Catherine Johnson and Barnaby Harsent.

Franc Roddam extends his thanks to Alan Yentob and Laura Mackie.

Dan Waddell would like to thank his agent Araminta Whitley and her assistant Celia Hayley for all their efforts.

Published by BBC Books, BBC Worldwide Limited
80 Wood Lane, London W12 0TT

ISBN 0 563 48720 8

Commissioning editor: Ben Dunn
Project editors: Catherine Johnson and Barnaby Harsent
Copy editor: Tessa Clark
Designed by M2
Picture research: Claire Parker
Production controller: Kenneth McKay

BBC Books would like to thank the following for providing photographs and for permission to reproduce copyright material. While every effort has been made to trace and acknowledge all copyright holders, we would like to apologize should there have been any errors or omissions.
All pictures courtesy of Carlton Television except for
Scope Features pp. 19, 25, 27, 37, 45, 47, 49, 52, 54, 55, 63, 64, 71, 97, 98 and 103; and Julia Tobin pp. 81–7.
Series 3 pictures © BBC.

Set in Bureau Grotesque, Monotype Baskerville, Stencil and Trixie
Printed and bound in France by Imprimerie Pollina, s.a. – L90885
Colour separations by Radstock Reproductions, Midsomer Norton

CONTENTS

01: DOWN THAT ROAD AGAIN

Pat Roach arrived first. Paranoid he would be delayed by traffic on his journey from Birmingham, he'd set off early, only to arrive half an hour before the appointed meeting time of one o'clock. The table at the Mirabelle, on Curzon Street in London's West End, had been booked in the name of Franc Roddam, the creator of *Auf Wiedersehen, Pet*, one of the best-loved and most successful shows in the history of British television. It was December 2000 and putative plans had been made to revive the series. The idea had drawn scepticism from several quarters, however, not least from several members of the cast and the show's writers, Ian La Frenais and Dick Clement. The lunch had been arranged to detect whether enough enthusiasm, and will, existed to justify its revival.

As Pat sipped his mineral water Franc Roddam arrived. The show's first two series had been made by the now defunct Central Television and screened across the ITV network. The year before, Roddam had heard a rumour that the rights to *Aufpet* had reverted to him. After digging the original contract from a dusty box in his house in Notting Hill, London, Roddam found this to be true. This in turn inspired the thought of another series and he began to mull over a few ideas in his head. A few weeks later, while leaving a bathroom shop in Notting Hill, he bumped into Jimmy Nail, who was leaving a guitar shop. He mentioned to Nail that he was thinking of bringing back *Aufpet*; unknown to him Jimmy, for other reasons, had also been considering an approach to Clement and La Frenais to revive it, perhaps as a one-off feature. Earlier that year, together with Tim Healy and Kevin Whately, Nail had performed a sketch as their *Aufpet* characters at a benefit concert for a fellow actor in Newcastle, and had been granted a riotous reception when he walked on stage as Oz. Realizing they were thinking along similar lines, Roddam and Nail decided to pool their ideas. Nail phoned the surviving cast members to gauge their enthusiasm for a reunion, while Roddam mentioned the idea to the BBC's Director of Drama and Entertainment, Alan Yentob, a personal friend. On behalf of the BBC Yentob expressed an interest. The idea had gained a foothold.

After Roddam, the rest of the *Aufpet* cast arrived one by one, all of them embracing, cracking jokes. Roddam remembers the warmth that began to fill the room. 'There was a real sense that everyone there liked each other; the atmosphere was incredibly positive. As soon as I saw them arrive, the delight in their faces at seeing each other, of this family being reunited, I knew immediately that it would happen and that it would be successful too,' he recalls.

The cast had remained firm friends ever since the last series of *Aufpet* had been filmed in 1985/6. Many of them were godfathers to each other's children or had acted together on different projects. But this was the first time for five years they had met under the aegis of the show that had launched each of their careers. Waistlines might have expanded, hair receded, grey hair sprouted and mineral water replaced beer as the drink of choice, but in 15 years nothing had dimmed their remarkable fondness for each other and the show.

The restaurant's other diners can be forgiven for being distracted from their artichoke soup by the familiar faces that sat down at the table: Timothy Spall, one of Britain's best actors, whose film and television career had seen him come a long way since he played Barry, the pedantic anorak from Birmingham; Kevin Whately, whose roles in *Inspector Morse* and *Peak Practice* had made him a household name and one of the country's most popular actors; Jimmy Nail, who had been catapulted from obscurity to stardom in his role as everyone's favourite lunk, Oz, and who had since sold millions of records as a musician, and starred in and written several television series; Tim Healy, ever present on British screens in a huge variety of drama and comedy roles since he made his mark as the ever dependable Dennis; Chris Fairbank, who modestly still considers himself a jobbing actor, albeit one who has appeared in films with Clint Eastwood; and Pat Roach, the giant Brummie wrestler who played Bomber, who has worked with Stanley Kubrick, Steven Spielberg and Arnold Schwarzenegger (who wrote the foreword for Pat's autobiography, *If*).

As the actors exchanged stories and reminisced, the final, and arguably most important, pair arrived: Dick Clement and Ian La Frenais. A legendary partnership, they had written *Porridge* and *The Likely Lads*, arguably two of Britain's greatest ever sitcoms, before writing *Aufpet*. Based in Los

Previous page: Ian La Frenais, Franc Roddam and Dick Clement reunited during the shooting for the third series.

Dick Clement (above) and Ian La Frenais, one of the most successful writing partnerships in British television history.

Angeles, they have continued to write films, TV series and sketches. Every day, Ian leaves his home to walk to Dick's house down the road, arriving at 9.30 sharp in order to start that day's writing. With several projects already on the go, there was absolutely no need for them to risk their formidable reputations on another series of *Auf pet*. When Roddam had first mooted a third series during a speculative phone call, Clement recalls that his reaction was overwhelmingly negative. 'Oh God no,' was my first thought. Swiftly followed by, 'That's a terrible idea.' La Frenais shared his doubts about the wisdom of 'doing it all again'. A few years earlier the pair had written a film called *Still Crazy*, a comedy about an ageing rock band that decided to reunite for a final British tour, only for all their old animosities and petty hatreds to return and for the group members to remember why they split in the first place.

It was only when Roddam and Nail had begun to produce storylines and concepts that their attitude changed, that the memorable characters they had invented two decades before began speaking in their heads once more, and the idea of rounding up this group of men after 15 years in the wilderness set their creative juices flowing. Soon their enthusiasm was resuscitated and the pair became convinced it could work, a feeling bolstered by the *bonhomie* and goodwill around that table in the Mirabelle.

It fell to La Frenais to play Henry V, to stir the troops on the eve of battle. Looking around the table he noted that no one was considering reviving the series from a position of desperation. 'None of us need the gig,' was the way he put it. The only reason they were there was out of their loyalty to, and love of the show and each other. He outlined the storyline as it stood and took questions from the company before ending with the words: 'I can promise you that if we decide to do this, it will be bigger and better than it ever was before.'

Sixteen months later, in April 2002, Episode 1 of the third series of *Auf Wiedersehen, Pet* was screened on BBC1 on a Sunday night and 11.7 million viewers tuned in to watch the show – an unbelievable 48 per cent of the possible audience. The critics rhapsodized about the quality of

Oz explains his dream at the beginning of the third series.

the script and the acting. No other programme has been away from the screen for so long and come back to such popular and critical approval. This was a show about a bunch of middle-aged, working-class men; there was no sex and little violence; the star character was a bridge in Middlesbrough, Yorkshire. It shouldn't have worked; undoubtedly, it did. The *Auf Wiedersehen, Pet* story, which everyone – cast and crew included – thought had ended once the filming of a traumatic second series had been concluded, had a dramatic new chapter, 25 years after the idea first suggested itself to a young northern film-maker, in a place as diametrically opposed to the gastronomic opulence of the Mirabelle as it would be possible to find.

02: BREAKING AWAY

It was 1977 and Franc Roddam's career was beginning to flourish. He had just directed *Dummy*, a one-off drama for ATV, which had won widespread acclaim. Buoyed by this success, he returned home to visit his parents and friends in Norton, Stockton-on-Tees. One of his friends was Mick Connell, a bricklayer, later to be best man at Roddam's wedding. Expecting to meet Mick and the others in their local, he was surprised to hear from the regulars that Connell and his pals were abroad. 'They've gone to Germany,' Roddam was told. When he asked why, he was told that work was so hard to come by that labourers from all over the northeast of England were being forced to seek work abroad. Britain's blue-collar base was being slowly eroded and the Labour Government was having little success in halting that decline. As Roddam saw it, a whole social group was in the process of being left behind. Immediately he sensed the dramatic potential of his friends' quest for work and when Mick Connell returned he was quick to find out about their life in Germany. 'Next time you go over there, I'm coming with you,' he told him.

A few months later he was on board a ferry on his way to Stuttgart in Germany with Mick and Mick's brother-in-law, who sent a postcard to his wife from the first service station they stopped at for petrol – a detail Roddam passed on to Clement and La Frenais who then incorporated it into the character of the terminally homesick and miserable Neville. But it was on the ferry that he began to collect the material he needed to shoot a drama.

'The night boat from Hull to the Hook of Holland had 35 guys from Teeside on it. The boat had a casino, so no one slept, everyone was drinking and gambling. There was one guy there who'd been to the same primary school as me. He was drunk and maudlin. "I've been married for 11 years," he said, "and this is the first night I've ever spent away from our lass." In this day and age that sounds strange but in those days the working man rarely spent a night away from home. This guy was in a state of real distress, in tears. I asked what he was going to do when he got to Germany. He said, "I'm going to sweep up in a paint factory." I couldn't believe it. This guy was a skilled craftsman, with three kids and who loves his wife. Yet here he was, having to leave them to find the most menial work. There was real sadness to him.'

By car, Roddam travelled with Mick to a railway station on the Dutch–German border where around 200 men from England were waiting for agents to arrive from Germany and hire them to work on sites. Mick, who was on his sixth visit to Germany and therefore knew the ropes, and his brother-in-law were billeted to work on a site in Stuttgart. Roddam went with them and spent two weeks there – living in a hut.

'It was an extraordinary experience. Guys living like they were in a prisoner-of-war camp. I'd been brought up on a diet of World War II movies and knew all the clichés. Here we were, with the pride of the British working force having to go over to Germany and live in Nissen huts, along with the Greeks and the Turks. The Geordies had become the Irish of Europe, living in huts, sharing accommodation and shower blocks. I just thought there was a tremendous irony about the children of the people who fought Germany going back to rebuild the country their dads and grandads had flattened – because their own country couldn't provide for them.'

In 1974 Roddam had directed what he describes as the first fly-on-the-wall documentary ever made, *The Family*, for which he spent nine months living with a British family. During that shoot he joined them on holiday in Majorca. It gave him an insight into how the British behaved abroad, how they packed their own food in a suitcase and how, when faced with a plate of paella, they ate everything including the seafood shells. In Germany with Mick and his mates he witnessed another clash of cultures, which he duly noted. On one occasion he went with the brickies to a state brothel.

'You imagine: you're from the northeast of England and suddenly you're confronted with a legal brothel. This one was down the side of a railway cutting and it was like a council block. The guys stood against the wall and the girls were brought out. This Irish guy who was with us went along the line and picked out the girl he wanted. Turned out she was Irish too. "Bloody hell, I've got an Irish one," he shouted. Next thing you know he was back out there with the rest of us. "That was quick," someone said. He said, "I've only got 40 Deutschmarks."

Previous page: Gary Holton and Ian La Frenais onsite during filming in Hamburg.

12

'On the other hand there was this big, aggressive guy, a sort of Oz character. He was in there for ages. We all waited for him outside and a few hours later he eventually made it out. We all asked him what happened. He told us: "She says to me, 'Do you want the special.' I said, 'What's that, like?' Then she put a saddle on me back and started whipping us with a riding crop. It bloody hurt. So I chinned her and they wouldn't let me out after that, like."'

The inherent humour of the situation was never far away, as you would expect from a group of men away from their wives and answerable to no one but themselves. Roddam remembers that, for those not inclined to be homesick, the life was a good one; sitting around drinking beer with your mates, watching the girls go by. Many of the men had married painfully young, often to the first girl they slept with. Suddenly, barely in their twenties, they had wives and kids and adult responsibilities. Then these same men found themselves in Germany ten years later with a wage packet and few responsibilities other than sending a few quid home. Having fun became an integral part of the experience; it was a chance to act like single men with no ties. Many returned home to their families older and wiser, extolling the virtues of German beer and asking for schnapps in their local pub, to the bewilderment of several landlords.

On his arrival back in England Roddam made straight for Willy Russell, an emerging new playwright, who later wrote classic plays like *Educating Rita* and *Shirley Valentine*. What Roddam had in mind was a hard-hitting 'play' in the tradition of the great BBC drama *Cathy Come Home*, with 'lots of sex, lots of music, lots of fun too, all the things that the working class love'. Russell expressed an interest in the story and, with Roddam, he went on a recce to Germany on Mick Connell's next expedition. The experience was not an inspirational one for Russell, according to Roddam, because his involvement ended on their return. The idea itself fell victim to its originator's success: *Dummy* had attracted the interest of the film world and Roddam was asked to direct *Quadrophenia*, the seminal film about disaffected youth in Sixties Britain, which would cement his reputation as one of the country's most arresting directing talents. Coincidentally, Timothy Spall and Gary Holton have their first film roles in that film, as the projectionist and aggressive rocker respectively. (For the trivially minded, *Auffpet* irregulars Michael Elphick and Ray Winstone also made their first impressions in *Quadrophenia*.)

For two years, until late 1979 when *Quadrophenia* went on general release, Roddam's idea about the brickies in Germany gathered dust. Yet he still retained an affection for it. No matter what he worked on, how glamorous the project was, it remained, nagging away at him all the time, asking him to do something about it. If anything, the election of Mrs Thatcher as prime minister in 1979 made the idea more relevant; more and more men were being forced to leave their lives and wives to find work elsewhere as recession bit deep into the core of Britain's manufacturing industry. But Roddam was about to enter possibly the busiest stage of his career. *Quadrophenia* had an immediate impact, even doing well in the United States. The *New York Times* hailed it as the best British film for 20 years and as a consequence Roddam found himself courted by Hollywood. With the prospect of a three-movie deal it became apparent, as 1980 rolled round, that he wouldn't be able to transform the builders' idea into reality. So he did what he considered the next best thing and decided to offload it on to people he trusted.

'Dick Clement and Ian La Frenais were heroes of mine. I loved *The Likely Lads*. I rang Allan McKeown who was a partner in their production company, Witzend, and told him I wanted to meet with Dick and Ian. I was living in Hollywood by then and they'd been out there for a few years.'

Clement and La Frenais had left Britain for Hollywood in 1975 to adapt *Porridge* for the American market. The pair had met in the early 1960s through a mutual friend at the London School of Economics. Clement, a southerner, was a BBC trainee; La Frenais, from the northeast, was unemployed after a stint selling cigarettes. As part of his BBC traineeship Clement was asked to direct something, so he and La Frenais decided to adapt a sketch they had written for a pub cabaret. It became *The Likely Lads* and from that point, their mastery of dialogue, of capturing the humour in everyday conversation and the wry, witty way in which people communicate, helped them to mould a comedy writing partnership that rivals Galton and Simpson as Britain's best.

Despite an initial lack of success for the *Porridge* remake, the pair remained in Hollywood writing for the movies, a departure marked by their scripting of full-length features for *The Likely Lads* and *Porridge* – which Clement also directed – and an adaptation of Anthony Hope's *The Prisoner of Zenda* for the big screen. Since *Going Straight*, the follow up to *Porridge* which saw Fletch doing just what the title said, they had not written much for British television, so they were intrigued when McKeown said Roddam had an idea he wanted to pitch.

The fateful meeting took place at the Café Moustache on Melrose Avenue, Los Angeles. Roddam explained the idea: how he knew of men from the northeast who were forced to leave their homes and families to work in Germany; how they lived in huts on top of each other in conditions reminiscent of a Stalag; how the men's northern working-class ways clashed with those of the locals. The pitch worked; Clement and La Frenais were enthused immediately. According to Roddam, La Frenais' response was to say, 'I love it so much I want to go back and start writing it this afternoon.' Dick Clement explains why:

'It's one of those ideas we'd never have found ourselves because we'd never know this was happening because we lived in LA. But instinctively it sounded good and right in our wheelhouse: men working abroad and the culture clash you have, and the fact they were ordinary guys too. The best television we'd done was always about guys struggling against the odds. But this was different; it was positive. These guys were taking action rather than just sitting around on their bums talking about it. We agreed to do it there and then.'

La Frenais was enamoured for the same reasons. That the programme would contain a serious social message and make a point was another attraction.

'The idea of doing something "right on" in a social context was nice. Britain in 1980/1981 might have been all right if you were one of the guys who drove around in a BMW. But under Mrs Thatcher there were a lot of people unemployed. These guys were among them, having to leave their families to go live in a hut in Germany. It gave the programme an edge. We didn't set out to be political, but the whole reason for these guys being where they were was political in a sense. It couldn't be ignored.'

Roddam handed over all his notes and research material, including the name of Mick Connell. Meanwhile, Allan McKeown approached ATV with the idea. Unbelievably, Charles Denton, its Head of Drama, said yes to the idea and commissioned 13 one-hour episodes simply on the strength of what he'd been told. As Franc Roddam acknowledges, the reputations of those involved made Denton's decision look less precipitate. He describes him as a dream for a director or producer.

'He's the sort of guy who, when you walk in a room and pitch an idea, says "Yes" or "No" straight away, and if he said "Yes" he meant it. It wasn't "Yes, I want to see a treatment," or "Yes, film me a pilot episode," it was "Yes, we're going to make this." He trusted us, pure and simple, though obviously it helped that Dick and Ian were so successful and that I was becoming a bit of a Hollywood hotshot. But it was still brave; he was paying out money for 13 shows and an unknown cast. Who would commission something like that now? They wouldn't.'

Good as this was, for Clement and La Frenais it meant they had to produce a first episode and some characters. To this end they started doing research of their own. La Frenais made a series of 'phone calls to Mick Connell, from Los Angeles to Stockton-on-Tees – an avenue of communication that became problematic when the Connell's telephone was cut off. Undeterred, La Frenais took to 'phoning a public telephone box down the street from Mick's house. At just before 1 a.m. GMT Mick would pull on his slippers and wander down to wait for the call. One night as he stood outside the box smoking a cigarette, a police car pulled up. Mick was known to them.

'What are you doing, Mick?' the policeman asked, winding down his window.

'Waiting for a call from Hollywood, officer.'

'Yeah, and the rest. C'mon, what are you really up to?'

Just then the 'phone rang. And the policeman, with a wary eye on Mick, picked up the receiver.

'Is Mick Connell able to take a 'phone call from Hollywood?' came the operator's voice. It was Ian La Frenais on the line. The officer beat a baffled retreat.

La Frenais, with Martin McKeand who was to produce the show, arranged to travel with Mick and his mates to Germany on Mick's next trip, to experience life on the building site at first hand. The group flew into Düsseldorf. As they went through passport control La Frenais heard the sound of a disagreement behind him. The German customs officials were in a heated exchange with Mick. Soon their 'guide' was surrounded by several angry-looking officials and led away for questioning. It emerged that Mick was a wanted man. On his last trip to Germany he'd borrowed someone's car and unfortunately driven it into a wall before doing a runner, so, as soon as he laid foot on the country's soil again, he was arrested in true efficient German style. A £400 fine was requested for his release, raised only by La Frenais and McKeand pooling the daily allowance they had planned to pay themselves. 'It was classic *Auf Wiedersehen*,' is how La Frenais remembers the incident. The rest of the trip was less productive.

'It was disappointing actually. We met hardly anyone apart from a few Irish guys. We'd imagined it to be flooded with British crews, except it wasn't, so in terms of picking up colour and seeing how they lived, it wasn't that prolific. What it was good for though was procedure: who hired these people, how they were hired, how they were paid, details like that. The most important thing then was to decide who the characters were.'

This was Clement and La Frenais's task in their office in Los Angeles. From what research they had done and what Roddam had told them, they decided the three principal characters should be Geordies. The name Oz came into Dick Clement's mind very quickly, he says, and he liked the fact it was only two letters and therefore easier to write in the days when their scripts were written in longhand.

'Then came the names Neville and Dennis, though from where I don't know. It grew from those three. But we knew we wanted them to be Geordies. For *The Likely Lads* we always hedged our bets as to where it was set. In those days there were very few actors who could "do" Geordie. With this series though, we weren't going to mess around: they were from Newcastle. Recently I looked back at the first handwritten episode and I noticed we said Neville was a good bit younger than the other two, which I think we must have conveniently ignored when it was cast, because all three of them were about the same age.

'Once we decided on those three characters the others just came along one by one. They started to speak to us. It's a strange thing when you create characters; sometimes they just happen, sometimes they don't. All of them are invented or are amalgams rather than real people. Barry just sort of happened, for example. The characters we created did cover the regions, though we wanted to avoid those Second World War movies where you have a Jock and a Taffy and those sort of stereotypes. We had three Geordies already, so we had to ring the changes for the others to reflect that working guys from all over Britain were going abroad. Part of where they come from depends on the accents Ian and I can do, because we do all the voices when we write. Ian can't do Australian at all, so if we write an Aussie character then I have to do the voice. The great thing about Britain is that it's rich in dialect and there is so much to choose from.'

The first episode began to take shape. The three Geordies leave their native Newcastle, on the way bumping into Barry, the pedantic anorak from West Bromwich, and Wayne, the cocky Cockney who attracts Oz's ire immediately. Our three heroes find work on a site in Düsseldorf, and on arrival are forced to live in a hut. The comedy of capture, of enforced claustrophobia, men living on top of each other in an unnatural situation, was one that Clement and La Frenais had mined successfully in *Porridge* and would be replicated in *Auf Pet*. According to Clement, doing their national service had given them an insight into life lived in a hut with strangers, with limits placed on the pleasures of life. The way in which men communicate, the humour and the tensions, the petty feuds and the camaraderie that develops, were all themes they had tapped into for *Porridge* and would become a memorable part of that first series of *Auf Pet*.

Yet, despite the obvious humour of the situation, neither writer ever saw the show they were starting to write as a comedy. After having had to work within the confines of a half-hour sitcom for so long, they felt liberated by the freedom of writing a series of one-hour dramas. They wanted the show to deal with contemporary issues, such as feckless men, like Oz, who treat their wives appallingly and don't send money home to their families. Whatever humour was there arose from the situation; it wasn't forced, so Clement says.

'If it was funny, it was funny, but we didn't feel like we had to strive for jokes artificially, to contrive situations to get a gag. There is a feeling in comedy that each page must have a laugh on it, so it was nice to get away from it and write something "real". Not that we wanted to be preachy or write a searing indictment of Thatcher's Britain. But the politics were there and that context was a good one in which to write.'

Yet, as both writers admit, neither of them would wish to be involved in a project that lacked humour. And while the programme had some political impact, while it did illuminate a section of Britain that was being left behind by Mrs Thatcher's increasingly divisive leadership, what most viewers revelled in was the interplay between the sprawl of characters and their verbal sparring. The comedy came from the vivid and memorable individuals Clement and La Frenais created, and it is a well-worn – because it's true – adage in the comedy-writing world that the best comedy comes from character. One has only to look at the best examples from the past ten years to see that this is the case – whether it's the petty psychosis of Steve Coogan's Alan Partridge or the epic delusion of *The Office*'s David Brent.

While the first scripts were being written ATV, soon to become Central Television, and Witzend had appointed Martin McKeand as producer, and he in turn hired the directors Roger Bamford and Baz Taylor to direct the show. Bamford had been working for the BBC on *Play for Today* and at first was unsure about *Auf Pet*, not having directed any comedy before. But after reading the two or three scripts that had been written at that point, he was persuaded:

'I thought it could work very nicely, and I thought it would be interesting to work with Dick and Ian. The first thing I was told when I got the gig was: "Fill it with big names and build the hut in the studio and make it." I think they were thinking of names like James Bolam, established actors like that. But I didn't think that was the right way of doing it. I thought it needed realism, so I made the conscious decision to go the other way. Martin, bless him, was OK about it and so that was the way we decided to go.'

'Jimmy Nail to Wardrobe, Jimmy Nail to Wardrobe.'

03: GOING TO GET IT RIGHT

At the beginning of 1982, when casting for *Auf pet* commenced, Tim Healy, then approaching 30, had just finished his first movie. Entitled *The World Cup: A Captain's Tale*, it told the *Boys' Own*, yet true story of the 1909 'world cup', when a British club team from West Auckland in Durham, beat Juventus in Italy to win the European club competition that later gave its name to the world's biggest sporting contest. The film was an *Auf pet*-esque tale of simple northern men exposed to sophisticated European society. It featured Dennis Waterman, Nigel Hawthorne and Dai Bradley (who would be considered for the part of Neville). Tim Healy's role was, in his own words, 'a little hard case who played full back'. Luckily for him, it was released just as Roger Bamford was issuing an all-points bulletin to his casting team to scour the country for every Geordie with an equity card.

Healy was firmly ensconced as a member of what was known to its recruits as the 'Geordie Mafia', a cabal of entertainers from the northeast that included the likes of Kevin Whately, 'Sammy' Johnson, Whately's wife Madelaine Newton, Val McLane (Jimmy Nail's sister) and several others. Despite appearing in repertory and turning up in episodes of *Crown Court*,

Emmerdale Farm and *Coronation Street*, Healy had spent ten years acting on the stage. Together with Newton and McLane, he was a founder member of Live Theatre, a touring company that staged new plays by new writers across the northeast, and which still exists now, based in a new theatre on Newcastle's redeveloped Quayside.

He was starring in a production of C.P. Taylor's last play, *Bring Me Sunshine, Bring Me Smiles* when Bamford took the train to Newcastle to see him. Furnished with a copy of *The World Cup*, in which Healy's character was an aggressive head case, Bamford initially intended to cast him in the role of Oz, according to Healy. The person earmarked for the role of Dennis was another member of the Geordie Mafia, George Irving, who later went on to TV success in the BBC's *Holby City*. Healy read for the part of Oz with Irving as Dennis. The next week he was called back to read again, this time with 24-year-old Timothy Spall. Bamford had already cast him as Barry, the first of the seven leading actors to be given his role in the series.

'I worked with Tim in *The Brylcreem Boys* and he was brilliant in it. I worked with him in something else before and I knew I wanted him in it. But there was a problem because when I was reading the script, I couldn't really see anything suitable for him. He's a Londoner, and the only Londoner was Wayne and that's not him at all. Then I thought, "Actually, he's married to a Brummie." I wondered if he could do it and, bless him, he was absolutely brilliant.'

Bamford saw more than 200 people while casting *Auf pet* – and says he never saw Healy as Oz; that he was always going to be Dennis. Anyway, after deciding on the two Tims he was utterly lost, he claims, as to who else to cast. Oz was providing him with the biggest problems. Enter Jimmy Nail.

The circumstances that surround Nail's entrance into the story have entered *Auf pet* legend. Nail, then 28, was known around the northeast for his outrageous performances with a band called The Crabs, which often involved him taking to the stage in a frock and hobnailed boots. According to Tim Healy, he was earning money by buying and selling houses in and around Newcastle, and was knocking down a wall around the corner from where auditions were being held. Nail's girlfriend, Miriam, heard of the auditions and said to him, 'Why don't you go along to be an extra? It's good money.'

Nail agreed and went along. When he walked in Bamford immediately knew he had his Oz: tall, uncouth and with a face that could sour milk at a glance, all missing teeth, a bashed-up nose and surly working-class contempt that was graphically illustrated by his first, famous words to the director: 'Get your skates on because my car is parked on a double yellow and I don't want to be here anyway.' Rather than read as an extra, Bamford asked Nail to read for the part of Oz.

'We were in a hall in a suburb of Newcastle. The panel was Martin, Barry Ford, Central's casting director, and me. We all took it in turns to ask the questions and when Jimmy came in I remember it wasn't my turn; I was sat on the left of the table. Jimmy came in fairly belligerently and sat down. He had an equity card from being in his band, I think. Anyway, for the first five minutes Barry and Martin were asking him questions and I just sat there watching him. For the first five minutes I could not understand one word of what he said. Not one word.

Tim Spall, the first of the seven to be cast.

'He glanced at me occasionally, or rather he stared straight at me. I was obviously looking back. Right at the end he said to me, "Do you realize that if you look at people in this town like that then you'll get your fucking head kicked in?"

'He left and Barry said, "Well, he was a bit aggressive," and put a stroke through his name. I said, "Hang on. He's probably the most interesting person we've seen." I couldn't understand a word he said but there was something there. Reluctantly the others agreed to see him again.

Healy was asked to come in and read with Nail. Looking at him, he remembered his face from somewhere. It was a while before he realized that the giant standing next to him was Val McLane's little brother, Jimmy Bradford.

'Jimmy came to pick her up from the theatre sometimes, though he refused to come inside. He just sat in the car saying, "I'm not going in there. All them actors are poofs." We never went out to say hello to him though, because he was a scary-looking lad.

'I read Dennis and he read Oz and he was brilliant. They sent him out and Roger said to me, "What do you think?" I said, "I think he's great." It might have been a good thing I said that or they might have cast George Irving as Dennis and I would have been out of it. They said to me, "How would you like to play Dennis?" It didn't bother me that I wasn't going to be Oz. I told them I'd love to.'

The next stage was a screen test for both Healy and Nail. Seats were reserved for them on a plane from Newcastle to London, where they were being put up for the weekend. Healy got an impression of Nail's carefree approach to a prospective acting career when their taxi pulled up outside his house.

'Jimmy was still in bed, sleeping off the night before. I had to knock him up and get his arse in gear. We got to the airport just in time to get the plane, but we had to run for it. Here I was sprinting through the airport panicking about missing the plane that was taking me to what I viewed as the biggest chance of my life. I was furious; Jimmy didn't even apologize. He wasn't taking it too seriously then. He said, "I'm just going to London for the weekend, for the holiday like."

'On the train back up to Newcastle I remember saying to him, "I tell you what, mate, you've got that part." He said, "I divven't care man. It's been a good weekend." We'd been put up in a hotel and we'd been to the pub and had a good drink and a game of darts and that was all Jimmy cared about really. But then about a week later I got a phone call from him. "Bloody hell, I've got the part, man." He was made up. Then we had to move down to London for the rehearsals and filming, so we packed all our stuff on to the roof of my Triumph Spitfire and headed off down the M1 to London.'

Bamford hadn't been sure that Nail would come to the screen test.

'I think he thought we were all a bunch of southern poofs. But he did turn up and I just knew that he was going to be very good. But I was getting a bit concerned at this stage, because I remembered them telling me to fill the show up with stars and here I was doing the exact opposite, casting a guy who'd never acted before and who no one could understand. I suppose I was going out on a limb but 20 years ago I was a bit more arrogant than I am now, I suppose. I wasn't even sure he was that bothered about getting the part, or if he was then he certainly didn't show it. But I decided to put him on the shortlist and then got Dick and Ian over to have a look at him. I told them I thought he was interesting.'

Clement still remembers clearly the day he first saw Nail:

'Roger and Martin asked us along to the rehearsal rooms. There was thinly veiled excitement in their voices that indicated they believed they were on to something. We walked in and I saw Jimmy immediately; well, you couldn't miss him. Before he even said a word, I leaned over to Ian and said, "Please God, let him be able to act," because he was Oz. When he opened his mouth it was obvious he was very, very raw, but then he had never acted in his life. And his Geordie accent was the thickest I'd ever heard. There were times in that first series, particularly with that slightly dodgy sound quality, where people said to me, "I can't understand him." But then neither could I, and I wrote the bloody thing. In a way, and with the benefit of hindsight, that added to the authenticity.

Kevin Whately, whose wife Madelaine suggested he go for the part of Neville.

'We learned his sister was an actress, which comforted us, made us think there might be something in his gene pool. But Jimmy was perfect for the part and that is the sort of thing that only happens once or twice in a lifetime.'

Nail got the part. Kevin Whately, meanwhile, had been snapped up for the role of Neville. Though he was based in London, he'd heard the rumour among the southern branch of the Geordie Mafia that a show had been written about men from the northeast and that the characters were being cast.

'We all wanted to be in it. I went to the first lot of interviews in London at Portland Square where the old Central Television offices used to be. I'd just finished being in a play called *Accounts* at the Hammersmith Lyric that had won a few awards. I'd played a youngster from the northeast in a pair of scruffy jeans, which got me recommended for an audition. I'd also been in a BBC thing about an archaeological dig, called *The Dig*. I got sent one or two scripts and the one thing that stood out immediately was the quality of the writing; it was certainly the best I'd ever read.

I could see the most interesting character was Oz, it was a glorious part, and it crossed my mind to go for that, but my wife, Madelaine, said, 'Go for Neville. Everyone will want to play Oz.'

Whately's wife was right. When he attended the audition many more actors were reading for the part of Oz than for any other, though few impressed Bamford. Whately, however, did. He went to Greenland to film *Shackleton* for the BBC and missed the screen tests for the part, and that impeded his chances of getting it. But Bamford eventually decided Whately was the right man.

'Neville was difficult to cast. I saw Kevin down in London but he wasn't an obvious one to start with. I had a list of about four or five possibles. I remember one of them was Dai Bradley, who was in *Kes*. I was quite keen on him as well. But there was a vulnerability to Kevin that appealed to me. I can't remember the details of the story, but he told me in his interview about this awful time working for an accountant's office in Newcastle and I thought, "Poor sod." I liked him and I went with that. He's the sort of person who you could imagine having a strong wife like Brenda, being a bit henpecked but always wanting to please. He came out brilliantly.'

With the Geordies and Tim Spall in place, Bamford moved quickly to fill the other parts. For the role of Bomber, the team plumped for Pat Roach. A wrestler, he was the only member of the cast who was known to the general public – or 'grapple fans', as Kent Walton, the commentator on wrestling for ITV's *World of Sport*, used to refer to viewers. Roach's size had led to him being cast as a heavy in several Hollywood blockbusters, and he was a particular favourite of Steven Spielberg. He appeared in *Raiders of the Lost Ark*; first as a German lieutenant who gets mangled in an aeroplane propeller and then as Otto the Sherpa who is plunged into a fire by Harrison Ford. While filming that huge-grossing film, his friend Ron Lacey told him about a new TV series that was being cast, and that the characters included a West Country man who Roach might want to consider playing. Confident he could hide his broad Brummie accent beneath a West Country burr, Roach auditioned for the part. In his view it went terribly.

'The bit I'd learned was no longer in the script. They gave me something else to read. It's the bit in the hut when Bomber is stripped to the waist polishing his shoes and young Neville is looking at his tattoos. Bomber notices him and says, "You looking at my tattoos lad?" Then he says, "These is nothing. My mate Jigger has got a whole fox running down his back and you can just see the fox's brush sticking out the crack of his arse." I just could not get it right, the dialect, all of it really. Then I was asked to read another bit, outside the brothel this time. I was meant to say the line, "Depends on what your proclivities are." And could I say the word proclivities? No, I couldn't. I looked at Roger Bamford who seemed to be the "Don't call us, we'll call you" type.'

Bamford did call him, and it was to offer him the part. Roach was dumbstruck. He claims his first reaction was to think, 'Do I want to work for people who are willing to hire me?' He agreed, even though he held out little hope of the show being a success. He says that when 13 episodes of scripts came through his letterbox he 'nearly died on the spot'.

'Even though Bomber didn't have that many lines it was still a lot for me to read and learn, considering I'd never really done that before. Until then I was always an action actor; I'd never done great exchanges of dialogue. In fact, I've never considered myself an actor. Instead I've

Former wrestler 'Big' Pat Roach grapples with the part of Bomber.

always seen myself as a bit of a usurper. I've just been a lucky guy who got a part in a few bits and pieces, and I never saw myself going any further than that.'

Bamford picked Roach because he knew the show needed a 'giant'.

'We needed a big man who was able to sort out the problems, simply with his physical presence most of the time. Pat is a very gentle man, but he was a wrestler at the time and he'd done a couple of Spielberg films. He came in, he read well, so I thought, "Let's give him a go." We were trying to make everybody different, have a contrast, so a huge, bearded man was ideal.

'We all used to give him a bit of stick about his wrestling, about it being rigged. But he denied it. I went down to film him wrestling for the credits for the second series. I said to him beforehand, "If you could just fall near the camera so I can see your face, that'd be great." Lo and behold, he fell right in front of the camera, in the perfect position. I'm not sure what that said about wrestling if something could be stage-managed that perfectly.'

Next to be drafted in was Gary Holton. Ian La Frenais first spotted him, somewhat incongruously, at a children's birthday party in London. He got chatting to him and as a result told Roger Bamford that he'd met someone who would make a 'perfect Wayne'. Holton, the lead singer with the Heavy Metal Kids, had performed cameos in cult films like *Quadrophenia* and *Breaking Glass*, but had done no television, although he'd sung the theme tune to *Murphy's Mob*, a children's show about a football team. Despite Holton's inexperience, Bamford agreed with La Frenais that he would be the ideal person to play the leering London Lothario, Wayne.

'Ian brought Gary to me, so I can't claim any credit for that. He pushed for him and he seemed right for the role, and who was I to argue with Ian because he knew what he was writing. And in many ways Gary was like Wayne. He was just right.'

'Gary was a lovely guy. It was funny really, because in the script there is tension between the Geordies and the Londoner, and there was a bit of that in real life, which was good for the show.'

The last of the main characters to be cast was perhaps the most underwritten. Clement and La Frenais had written Moxey for their friend Ray Cooper, a member of Elton John's backing band who liked the idea of trying to act. Because they didn't know how good he would be, his part was deliberately sketchy. When Cooper was unable to make the audition the role became free, and one of the young actors who auditioned was Chris Fairbank.

Fairbank, then aged 29, knew Kevin Whately from a production of *Romeo and Juliet* in Newcastle which they had both appeared in and Whately and his wife lived near Fairbank in Tooting Bec. One Sunday afternoon in the early summer of 1982 Whately paid him a visit to tell him, breathlessly, that he'd been cast in a new show about Geordie brickies, and advised his friend to get his agent on to it. At this stage Fairbank was becoming disillusioned with acting after being fired from a 60-week contract with the Royal Shakespeare Company because of a disagreement with a director. He'd already terminated his acting career once before. After a few years in repertory he decided it wasn't for him, travelled across North Africa, spent a year as a deckhand and was shipwrecked before eventually deciding to return to England and have another go at acting. Until he was bundled out of Royal Shakespeare Company it had been going well, with the odd TV part coming his way and a role in Ken Campbell's 9½-hour science-fiction epic, *Illuminatus*.

Fairbank had no need to call his agent because only a few days after Whately's visit she called him, to tell him to go to an interview with Martin McKeand, Roger Bamford and Dick Clement. One look at the scripts told him there wasn't much for him to go on.

'Dick told me they weren't too sure about Moxey's character. They didn't have too much idea about who he was, other than they thought it might be good if he was a bit sickly and always had a cold, not what you imagine a builder to be. He said to me, "Have you any thoughts?" I said, "From what I've heard, you've three Geordies, a Brummie, a Cockney, a West Country character. How about a Scouser? I lived there when I was a teenager for a couple of years. I could give you a bit of Liverpool." Dick said, "Yeah, give us a bit of that. We're thinking Irish but Liverpool sounds OK."

'It was at the interview that Dick came up with Moxey's first punchline. They thought he would come in with the dartboard, which is basically how he gets in the hut. But Dick said,

Gary Holton, who got the part of Wayne after meeting Ian La Frenais at a children's party.

"Actually, a good line would be if he said, 'But I haven't got any darts.' Stick that in at the end." So I read it and that was it.'

A couple of days later Fairbank was called by his agent to say he'd got the part. She wasn't keen for him to take it, for good reason.

'Pippa knows me very well and how bored I get and how quickly I get bored. One of the fast tracks to boredom is not having enough to do. It's not an ego thing: I just get bored. In her view there wasn't enough to keep me interested. I said to her that only two episodes had been written, but she felt that the three Geordies were the main characters, and that Tim Spall was already involved. "They haven't got enough screen time to develop more than that," she said. "You'll be on the periphery." But she also understood where I was coming from and how desperate I was to work, to feel I was still in the game. She was just warning me. I believed I would act my way into the frame; it would be a challenge.'

Bamford liked the contradictions in Fairbank. As he points out, anyone meeting him recognizes them immediately. From Fairbank's diminutive body emerges a rich, resonant, 'actorly' voice that surprises those expecting Moxey's weedy, stuttering Scouse accent.

'I saw so many people for Moxey, actors of all sorts. But Chris is this chirpy guy with his wonderful deep voice that doesn't seem to fit. I just warmed to him. He was different, in many ways, and that was what I was after for Moxey.'

Tim Healy tells how he was drinking with Fairbank in a pub when a fan approached them.

'This guy said, "Can I have your autograph, Dennis?" Then he said, "Can I have yours too Moxey?" Chris said [Tim adopting a deep bass voice], "Of course you can." This guy looked at him, amazed, and said, "You're not Moxey." "No," Chris drawled. "I play the role."'

So Bamford had his unknowns – Pat Roach was the most famous of the seven, and that was because of his wrestling not for any acting he had done. He acknowledges that had he been asked to cast the roles in 2003 the programme would have been completely different.

'I would not have been able to cast any of those seven now. Not one of them. I would have been told who to cast, or given a choice of people I could cast. I don't know how people find actors today. But then the whole show might not have been made today; there certainly wouldn't be 13 episodes, and it wouldn't have had a chance to build. It wouldn't have set new ground, which it did.'

With the seven main characters established, all that remained was to recruit actors for the supporting cast. One of these was Julia Tobin, who played Neville's wife, Brenda, the only female to appear in every series. She hails from the northeast but was living in London when she heard rumours of the series. She had only acted in the theatre, but she decided to submit a letter and photograph, and was asked to audition. She was given the part and the next thing she remembers is being asked to attend a read-through with the other members of the cast. No one can remember the venue for this first meeting, other than that it was a dusty church hall or village hall. Tobin does remember what happened.

Chris Fairbank, whose idea it was to make Moxey a Scouser.

Julia Tobin, the only ever-present female in the series.

'I remember us reading all the episodes and everyone being there, all the actors. We sat in one gigantic circle and everyone introduced themselves. I think a few people knew each other already, but for everyone else it was still quite new, quite nerve-racking. Kev Whately and I had been at the same drama school so we knew each other. He was in his last year when I joined. That made it a bit easier considering I was playing his screen wife. But we started reading and within seconds people were laughing, really, really laughing and it was fabulous.'

04: WORKING ON THE SET FROM MORNING 'TIL NIGHT

When filming of the first series of *Auf Wiedersehen, Pet* began in August 1982 all the scripts had not yet been written; Bamford estimates only five or six were complete. Clement and La Frenais had written the first three together, then Clement was offered the chance to direct a feature comedy, *Bullshot*. La Frenais was faced with having to write the rest of the series himself, so help was needed. Stan Hey had written a sitcom about a Cockney hairdresser, which Witzend had piloted for ATV and which starred Tracey Ullman, who later became the wife of Allan McKeown, Witzend boss and *Aufpet* executive producer. The outbreak of the Falklands conflict scuppered any chances the show had of reaching the screen, but it impressed Clement and La Frenais sufficiently for them to ask Hey to contribute a script to their new series. He wrote episode five, which gave Bomber the main storyline with his runaway daughter ending up in the lads' care.

Appropriately, the first location was Germany, which involved a three-week shoot in Hamburg – though the series was to be set in Düsseldorf, a suitable building site that was halfway through construction had been found there for the external shots. The site would be re-created, brick by

brick, on the back lot of Elstree Studios in England (the lot that was later turned into Albert Square for *EastEnders*) where the rest of the series would be filmed. While in Hamburg, the crew also shot scenes that were supposed to take place on the streets of Düsseldorf (the trainspotting tendency among some fans led them to spot Hamburg number plates on cars that pass the actors in these scenes).

Spirits among the cast were buoyant; everyone was excited to be away from home and embarking on such an adventure together. Not unlike the characters they played. Occasionally, high spirits turned more boisterous as La Frenais, who joined them for the first week, recounts.

'I was out there and the guys went pretty wild. I suppose the nicest way of putting it was that they got into character. There was a lot of pubbing and clubbing, and occasionally it got out of control. It was a mixture of nerves and bravado and no serious damage was done. The police were called to the hotel on the odd occasion but it was nothing really. The guys were strangers embarking on a great adventure.

'While I was there Gary Holton and I went to have a serious talk one night, because I knew his wife, Susan. We went to this bar that seemed suitably quiet and ordered a bottle of Blue Nun. While we spoke this couple came out and started having sex on the floor beside us. It was bizarre because we were so wrapped up in our conversation we hardly noticed. We laughed at the incongruity of it all but we just carried on. When we left we bumped one of them on the leg as

Left: The back lot at Elstree before the set was built. Right: Building starts ...

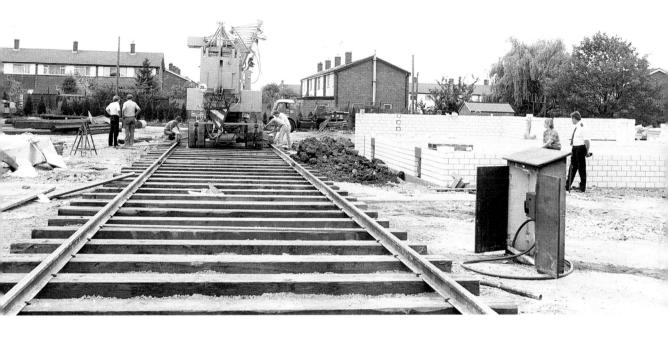

we got up and I remember saying sorry, but they didn't pay us much attention either. It was the most expensive bottle of Blue Nun ever.'

Alcohol had already played a part during some of the first scenes shot. On their way to Hamburg, Nail, Healy and Whately were filmed as their characters, journeying through Holland to Germany. *En route* one of the drivers fell ill, so they arrived later than planned to film the scene in which Herr Pfister hires them to work on the Düsseldorf site. The venue for this scene was filled with members of the British army, who had been hired as extras. Unfortunately, the delay in the actors' arrival gave the soldiers time to refresh themselves liberally at the expense of Central Television, drinking more than 600 bottles of beer between the 70 of them present. By the time Whately *et al.* arrived it was becoming increasingly difficult to control them. After several takes and intervals while yet another drunken squaddie was hauled off the floor, the scene was finished.

The convivial atmosphere continued throughout the three weeks in Germany. The local police, it would be diplomatic to say, were not strangers to the actors' Hamburg hotel, and once chased two members of the *Auffpet* contingent through its corridors until they sought sanctuary in a cupboard – which was then dismantled. In another incident the *polizei* were called when a member of the cast became embroiled in a heated debate with the president of a local football club. Chris Fairbank admits his recollection of that period is somewhat hazy. 'We all liked a few beers back then. Some more than others. I was one of the "somes".' What he can recollect is that during a few of those lengthy sessions at the bar in the Intercontinental Hotel a few of the holes in Moxey's mysterious past came to light.

'Ian La Frenais has a mind like a tape recorder. He will sit there and be part of the conversation, and if someone says something he'll sit back and listen. You won't think anything of it until you're reading the script and you say, "Hang on, I was talking about that the other night." I told him about my past. My connection with Liverpool was a spell in a probation hostel when I was 17, for smoking dope. That might have been part of their reason for making him an ex-con, perhaps.'

Another venerable *Auf pet* anecdote was forged during attempts to film the infamous brothel scene for the first episode. For the sake of authenticity it was shot in Hamburg's red-light district and German prostitutes were brought in to add some local colour.

'You wouldn't have got the same look with actors,' Kevin Whately says. 'But it was a strange atmosphere because although the girls were fine, there were some really terrible-looking women, which was great for the sake of authenticity, but their pimps were there too and they were really creepy characters.'

Not all the girls were what they appeared to be, as one unfortunate member of the *Auf pet* team discovered to his embarrassment. Deciding that it would be a bit of a waste to say goodbye to the girls once filming ended, he thought he'd befriend one of the loitering *Fräuleins*. Only to discover that the *damen* was in fact a *herren*. It brings a whole new meaning to the *Auf pet* lyric 'Going out on a bender'.

Roger Bamford remembers everyone's shock.

'It wasn't until after we filmed that we discovered some of the women were actually men. They were transvestites. We truly didn't know. We found this wonderful brothel and we thought all the women we'd bussed in were just that: women. It came as a bit of a shock for us when it came to light they weren't.'

For Jimmy Nail the almost overnight change in his circumstances, transformed from an average working stiff to a well-paid actor on a major television production, was difficult to digest, as Tim Healy remembers.

'He couldn't believe he was doing this as a job. He'd never done anything like it before. To go straight in as one of the leads in this programme baffled him a bit. To have people holding an umbrella over his head when it started raining, well, it was just a real shock for him. For the first three or four weeks he was on a high, he was getting drunk, he'll tell you that himself, but then he calmed down and got on with the job.'

Roger Bamford says it took some time for Nail to settle down, and even then he was still 'totally unpredictable'.

'He enjoyed himself and it took him a while to get used to it. But underneath, though he certainly wouldn't admit he was like that then, he was actually quite an old pro. He's pretty shrewd, but he'd been taken out of his environment and it was like giving a kid sweets. Here he was off to Germany, being paid for it, and he made the most of it.'

... and shooting begins.

Another legendary *Auf pet* tale told by some members of the cast, and both Ian La Frenais and Dick Clement, has Nail eating his dinner in the hotel with Tim Spall and a few of the other actors. 'I can't believe I'm doing this,' he kept repeating. 'Getting paid to lark around, do a bit of acting, have a drink in the bar after work. It's unbelievable.' Spall looked at him and said, 'You're home, mate.' While to some this might appear suspiciously like 'luvvie speak', it is said to have had a profound impact on Nail. He finally realized that here was a job he could do, where he was accepted for who he was, and where no one was going to turn round and tell him to change.

Once they had finished filming in Hamburg – though it was necessary for the actors to return when the whole series had been shot, to complete certain scenes – the cast and crew returned to London, via the real Düsseldorf where a few additional ones were filmed. Pat Roach took a room at the YMCA in Russell Square and Tim Healy and Jimmy Nail stayed with friends, while the others already lived in London. Before shooting got under way the cast were given a practical course in bricklaying, learning the rudiments only.

Filming started at Elstree in the autumn. A scale replica of the Hamburg construction site had been designed and built in the back lot. Producer Martin McKeand arranged for several tonnes of building material to be imported from Germany – there is apparently a marked difference between an English brick and a German one. Four wooden huts and a German portable toilet were also brought in for added authenticity.

One of those huts became the actors' 'home' for the next nine months. Also for the sake of authenticity, Bamford decided to ignore convention, which dictated shooting in a warm, comfortable studio, and filmed inside the hut. So, a huge studio stood empty as each morning the cast and crew traipsed through it and outside to a cold hut. People working at Elstree started to wonder who the scruffy characters were, who every day disappeared to a hut on a half-formed building site. Bamford believes it brought the cast together.

'It helped them gel, I think, because they were working in that hut almost every day. And there were tensions, there were arguments, people didn't always get on, which was great because it all came out when they acted. But it also drew everyone together. I took them in there and gave them their beds, said that's yours, that's yours and so on. They all got used to what was in their lockers. It was bloody freezing in there. Half an hour before everyone arrived in the morning someone went in to turn the stoves on because that was the only way to heat it. The seven of them would come in and sit on their beds, someone would make a cup of tea and then we'd work out some scenes. We lived in that hut and we bonded. Had we tried to do it in a studio it wouldn't have worked; it would have been too warm, too comfortable and we were striving for realism. I suppose I was pushing my luck a bit though, but I was determined to make it work.

'In a way it was easier to film because I could get rid of the multicamera nonsense. I said I wanted one camera and I could just structure all that. Because we had the building site I took them outside. We did have to remember that someone would turn a corner and they might be in the stuff we shot in Germany. The logistics were difficult in that respect. Hamburg was used for the wider shots, but there was a small area when they went around the corner and that was Elstree.'

This constant switching between what was filmed on the site in Hamburg and the lot at Elstree explains why Tim Spall often walks round a corner weighing eleven stone and emerges on the other side three stones heavier. According to Bamford, by the end of the shoot Spall couldn't fit into the costume he'd been wearing at the start of filming.

The convivial atmosphere fostered in Germany had not been lost. The producers had done a deal with Scottish and Newcastle Breweries, who had recently started importing the German beer Becks. Crates and crates of the drink were brought on to the set. For a group of thirsty young actors it was too much to resist. Tim Healy recalls.

Above right: Gary Holton takes a well-earned break from the hectic filming schedule.

w: The lads gather in the hut, which was to be their 'home' for the next nine months.

'For the first fortnight at Elstree we were drinking it solid. Then it dawned on us that you can't work well under those conditions; you can't act with a bellyful of beer – not that well, anyway. When we realized that we went on to fake pints.'

But any abstemious behaviour did not last long. Until lunch time to be precise. Then, according to Chris Fairbank, the gang would 'hit the bar'. Fairbank was travelling in every morning in Kevin Whately's Ford Granada, complete with 12-track stereo and, *Auf pet* folklore has it, a pair of old, dirty white underpants, which Whately used to clean his windscreen, in the glove compartment. Somehow the underpants ended up in Jimmy Nail's possession and, sensing a chance to get further into character, he began wearing them in the hut to emphasize Oz's slobbery. Oz's voluminous, grey underpants would become as familiar piece of TV clothing as Doctor Who's scarf or Paul Daniel's hairpiece.

Whether Fairbank got a lift back depended on how long the company spent in the bar after the day's filming was done. Working on the set all day, covered in brick dust and mud, then drinking in the bar in their filthy clothes earned the actors and some crew members a reputation around Elstree. Fairbank says they became pariahs.

'Word was going around Elstree that Central wouldn't be there for much longer because the TV franchises were up for renewal, and if they retained theirs they might have to move to the Midlands. I don't think anyone at Elstree knew what to make of us at all. I'm sure they weren't certain whether we were actors or if, in fact, we were builders and our building site was an actual construction for the benefit of whoever was going to take over from Central. We acted quite differently from the way actors behave now; we were in the bar at lunch time, in the evening. It was enormous fun.'

Kevin Whately says the *bonhomie* made for a sociable and pleasant working environment, even if the company's behaviour upset some of the more conservative elements at Elstree.

'We slobbed around Elstree. We were loud – well, Jim was loud. We were often in the bar. And we did daft things. Nothing too bad. We used to park in the Head of Light Entertainment's parking space. We didn't understand why anyone would have their own space. Generally, we got up people's noses.'

The mood of the crew members was influenced by the actors. Whately says the crew saw them joking around and playing practical jokes, and joined in. On one famous occasion they stitched Whately up. He was filming a scene in bed with Julia Tobin, in which she flicks through *Cosmopolitan* bemoaning their sex life while he tries to listen to football on the radio. Normally a soundtrack of a football commentary would have been dubbed on afterwards. Instead, the soundmen played a tape that Whately could listen to, and sneakily cued it to a point where Newcastle, Whately's team, scored. 'They scored and I didn't know what to do, because I was thinking the audience would be hearing it and therefore I should react in some way. I kept thinking, "Keep acting, keep acting," and I just lost it. I didn't know what to do.'

The out-take would make several appearances on shows of TV bloopers, keeping Denis Norden and his ilk amused for years afterwards.

The only person not to join in the carousing was Pat Roach. Not because he wasn't invited to, but simply because he was in the middle of a period of nine years without alcohol; keeping fit was his drug of choice. In the mornings, when the rest of the cast were arriving bleary-eyed and hungover, Roach would already be in the backlot going through his daily routine of 1,000 squats after an early morning swim. To maintain his energy for training and acting he was eating, he says, four porterhouse steaks every day.

One of the reasons for this fitness regime was to keep in shape to wrestle. When Roach signed up to play Bomber he was told to stay away from the ring while the programme was being filmed, for the reasonable fear that he would be injured. However, he couldn't resist the occasional grapple.

'Roger Bamford would say to me while we were filming, "You're not wrestling are you?" I'd say, "No, boss." But as filming progressed he'd be watching the TV on a Saturday and there I was, wrestling. On the Monday he'd come in and tell me that he'd seen me. "That was recorded," I'd say. This kept going until Roger would just look at me and say, "Recording eh?" and I'd nod. Eventually he just gave up and asked me for tickets.'

Roach wasn't only moonlighting as a wrestler; he was taking the opportunity to extend his movie repertoire. *Never Say Never Again* was being filmed in another part of the Elstree studios, and Roach obtained permission to nip across for a day to play a role in which he performs a lengthy fight scene with Sean Connery. When he reported for filming the first people he bumped into were Dick Clement and Ian La Frenais, who were doing rewrites for the movie.

In the latter stages of filming *Auf pet*, Steven Spielberg came to Elstree to shoot scenes for *Indiana Jones and the Temple of Doom*. Pat was given the role of Chief Guard, in which he meets yet another grisly fate – mashed in a stone-crusher during a fight with Indy. The shoot overlapped with *Auf pet*, and Roach gained permission from the long-suffering Bamford to leave the set for a day. He was told he must report back for six o'clock that evening to film the scene where the hut is burned down.

'I went over to the *Indiana Jones* set and said to the first assistant director, "Whatever happens I have to be back over there at six." Because of the scene I was shooting, on the conveyor belt, there was a make-up girl who kept having to 'black' me down because the stuff kept rubbing off while we were shooting the fight. I needed help from someone to scrub it off in the shower, too. On this day it got nearer and nearer to six o'clock. A few minutes before six there was a "cut" and I realized I didn't have time for a shower. I had this big, black beard on and I was blacked down. I ran across the road and I wasn't sure security would let me past. I went past the gate expecting to be stopped. The guard didn't even look up from his TV, he just said, "Evening Pat".

'I reported in and they said, "It's all right Pat, we're breaking for supper." They were taking the crew photograph though, which is why I appeared in it blacked down. So I went and had a shower and spent ages scrubbing all of the make-up off. When I came out supper had finished, I'd missed it. I walked over to the hut and someone said, "Pat, you need to go to make-up and be blacked down." They wanted us covered in soot for the fire scene. I couldn't believe it.'

Filming in the hut, not a studio, caused cramped conditions for cast and crew alike.

Everyone speaks of the wonderful atmosphere on the set and how well the seven main actors got on. None of them were household names, Roach aside – but his fame was a consequence of his wrestling career, a form of acting though far removed from the skills required by a television drama. The absence of a star prevented problems with swelling egos or actors becoming moody and uncooperative because they haven't been given sufficient lines, that often beset large-scale productions. Along with sharing a similar level of television-acting experience, or lack of it, the actors were similar in age and were at the same stages in their lives; during the series Spall became a father for the first time, while Whately, Holton and Nail had their first children towards the close of filming or shortly after it ended. This kept the group in touch once work on the series finished, meeting at an endless round of christenings and birthday parties. More importantly, they respected each other as men and as actors, and weren't frightened to suggest their own improvements to the script, as Fairbank remembers.

'Jimmy would improvise and stick lines in. He became inspired by things that Oz would definitely say and those crept in. It kept you on your toes. Many actors find that disturbing; if it's not in the script you don't say it. But this was exciting stuff. It felt as if we were rewriting the acting rule-book. Dick and Ian write brilliant scripts, but they don't mind if you just tweak it a bit and make it more you. If you've got a good line then bang it in, was their motto. If it doesn't work then nothing's said; you know it doesn't work so you don't do it again. It makes for a fantastic working environment.'

Credit must go to Roger Bamford for fostering that working environment. Many other directors, when confronted with an untried, untested bunch of young actors intent on enjoying themselves, would have tried to exert some discipline and ended up disagreeing with, or alienating, many of them in the process. Instead, Bamford chose to harness their energy and genuine love of the material to extract a series of brilliant performances.

'There was no point in trying to crack the whip; it was a case of moulding what I had. In a way I didn't want to discipline them because the interaction between the guys was very real, and had I tried to lay the law down that might not have developed. Whether the camera was on or off, there was always a lot of banter between them, always a lot of humour and winding-up.'

There were few problems and the entire nine months of filming is a fond memory for everyone involved, cast and crew. For Kevin Whately it was an unforgettable experience.

'From day one we all got on like a house on fire. We had lots of time to rehearse, to mess around, and to do a lot of drinking. No one stamped on us; Roger was great and he used all the energy we had, rather than trying to lay down the law.

'While we did spend a lot of time in the bar we knew our lines and carried on enjoying ourselves like we did in rehearsals, and I think the crew clued into that and they really enjoyed themselves too. It sounds too good to be true, but everyone really did get along well. There was never any fighting for position, trying to outdo each other; we just made each other laugh. The thrill of having these great scripts to do, and the fact that in those days TV was far more leisurely to do, all contributed to how well the filming went.'

It was a long shoot; long enough for Julia Tobin to contract meningitis, recover and return to the set without her absence interrupting the schedule. Roger Bamford and the crew sent her a bunch of flowers while she was in hospital. It was also long enough for Ray Winstone to win the inaugural *Auf Wiedersehen, Pet* award for the longest time ever taken to shoot a guest role in a TV series. Chris Fairbank still marvels at the length of time Winstone spent shooting his part as Colin, the runaway squaddie, in Episode 8.

'Nine months he was on it. He was there in Hamburg at the very start and he kept coming back. We named it the Ray Winstone award if ever one guest actor ended up coming back for months on end. No one broke his record though. If someone reappeared, we'd say, "Going for the Winstone award are you? You've another six months to go…" His span lasted almost as long as mine.'

Despite the fond memories the company has of its time at Elstree and in Germany, the shoot was not without mishap – most notoriously when Chris Fairbank fell down the stairs of his flat in London and broke his leg. Fortunately for the production it was towards the end of the schedule, but it meant that many scenes had to be shot with Moxey in a chair, his recuperating leg hidden by another member of the cast or a piece of furniture. In the scenes leading up to the immolation of the brickies' hut, Bomber is carrying a drunken Moxey. This was created out of necessity – Fairbank couldn't walk, so his screen character was rendered legless by alcohol. In the crew photograph that shows a blacked-down Pat Roach, Fairbank can be seen perched on crutches.

As filming progressed towards its close, there was no final episode. La Frenais was busy catching up on other episodes so Roger Bamford rang Stan Hey and asked him to write it. Hey wasn't given long.

'Roger called me and said they needed a final episode, one in which the lads were brought home from Germany. Circumstances had changed – the loophole allowing foreign workers to work in Germany tax-free had ended in 1981 or something, so we needed to bring the programme up to date. Roger said he wanted the script for the following Tuesday and this was Thursday evening. I was single then, so I just locked myself in my bachelor flat with a few cold tins of ravioli for sustenance and got stuck in.'

Nothing was said at this stage about the likelihood of another series so Hey's job was to tie up the loose ends. His main dilemma was whether Dennis should stay with Dagmar or go back to England to resurrect his and Vera's marriage. Hey plumped for the latter, and even wrote a scene in which Dennis and Vera are reunited, which was filmed but failed to make the final cut.

He also had to contend with the usual incidents and accidents that seem have to been visited upon the series over the years.

'I was halfway through the second draft when someone called to say, "Oh, Chris Fairbank has broken his leg." So I had to do a rewrite so that he never stood up, or he got so drunk that he had to be carried by Bomber. It was a show like that. You'd be there working on a draft and the phone would go, and it would be the story of someone hurting themselves, or in rehab, or someone being arrested. [Laughs] I'm joking of course, but something always cropped to keep you on your toes as a writer.'

What was decided before Hey's weekend vigil was that the hut would be burned down. Hey had spoken to both La Frenais and Bamford and had learned from them that the hut was despised by cast and crew, and that once the series had finished filming the set would be destroyed because Central was leaving Elstree and the BBC was moving in. So the idea of the fire developed from there.

It was a scene the seven actors were looking forward to. On Bamford's insistence, for the best part of nine months they had found themselves idling away time in that confined space, like the characters they were playing. Over the winter months it had proved both damp and cold. Sand from the set was brought in on the actors' shoes, and got in the beds in which a number of scenes were set. By the end of filming the hut didn't smell too pleasant either. So everyone was relishing the prospect of it being burned down. Except for Pat Roach. He saw what the special-effects men were doing and didn't like the look of what was being prepared – he was a man who had witnessed several large-scale stunts in his movie career. The resulting explosion was spectacular, according to Chris Fairbank.

'Special-effects guys can get carried away. To say the least. They were preparing this explosion, setting these devices but they didn't take account of the backdraught it would cause.

Above: The lads rejoiced in burning down the hut after nine cold, uncomfortable months. Inset: The smouldering wreckage the morning after.

The door from the hut was open at the start of the sequence. There was an interior shot of Barry's motorbike, which caused the fire. The backdraught caused the door to shut, so there was no way out. Smoke was everywhere. I think Ray Simper, the cameraman, lost most of the hair on his arms and legs, even his eyebrows. Everyone had to jump out of the windows.

'We'd been told to stand a safe distance away but, even from where we were, there were bits of burning debris flying everywhere. Let's just say the special-effects team surpassed themselves. None of us were too disappointed to see that hut burn, though. We were bloody glad to see the back of it.'

In a crane above the actors even Bamford felt the heat from the blast.

'That hut had been part of our lives for the best part of a year but no one was sad to see it go. I can't remember, but I suspect that in the meetings I had with Stan in the middle of the night about that last episode I might have said, "For God's sake, burn that bloody hut down." When it blew up, I was a long way above it and it nearly knocked people off their feet. The actors were dancing around the hut and they had to run from it; none of it was acting. Health and Safety would have gone mad now.'

When the scene was in the can and shooting had ended, there was an end-of-series party during which Stan Hey was thanked for his contribution and presented with the script of his episode, complete with Polaroids, which cemented his position as part of the team.

Once a wrap was called, the cast and crew were wistful. First, an enjoyable, unforgettable experience had ended; second, there was no belief whatsoever that they would be doing the show again. That they would remain friends was certain, but the chances of them acting together in the future, all seven of them, were unlikely to say the least. A few members of the crew had told the actors they believed the series might be a success – Whately remembers many of them laughing during the filming of the funnier scenes, always a good sign – but no one believed them, least of all Chris Fairbank who, because his character was the least well drawn, felt the least integrated into the group.

'I truly thought that was it when the job finished. I didn't think it would be a hit. My thought was, "Who the fuck is going to be interested in life on a building site in Germany? Who's going to watch it?" In many ways I didn't feel part of that first series. I was on the periphery a bit. Moxey had little to do or say. He always seemed to be lurking around the teapot or sneezing. Or he'd wander off and then come back and wander off again. So when filming finished I thought I was back to square one; a jobbing actor looking for work, worrying whether I'd done my last job. I never, ever, thought for a million years we'd do it again.'

05: HELPLESS HEROES CAUGHT IN A DREAM

In October 1982 the most powerful drama since *Cathy Come Home* appeared on British television screens. Like *Cathy*, Alan Bleasdale's *The Boys from the Blackstuff* shone an unflinching light into a corner of British society traditionally neglected by the mainstream media. The series had begun life as a one-off play in 1980 and the BBC had commissioned a six-part series for 1982. Following the lives of disenfranchised, unemployed men in a Liverpool decimated by Thatcherite policies and the demise of Britain's manufacturing base, the programme's almost documentary air of grisly realism had an immediate impact on the British viewing public and critics alike. In Yosser Hughes, superbly portrayed by Bernard Hill, Bleasdale had a character who resonated with the public; his plaintive plea of 'Gissa job. I can do that,' was imitated countrywide.

In dealing with dislocated, working-class men and their attempts to keep their heads, and those of their families, above the poverty line *Blackstuff* and *Aufpet* shared a similar theme. Because *Blackstuff* came before *Aufpet* – in terms of when it was screened; as we know, Franc Roddam first had his idea more than half a decade earlier – *Aufpet* was inevitably compared to it. However, all the programmes shared was a theme. While *Blackstuff* was angry and unremittingly bleak, alleviated only by a few shafts of black, mordant wit, *Auf pet*'s appeal was based on its verbal humour and the occasionally farcical situations in which the characters found themselves. While *Blackstuff* was transparently attempting to indict modern Britain, the politics of *Auf pet* were less forceful. Few, if any, of the characters were overtly political. Dick Clement believes the two programmes defy comparison, though many critics were unable to resist comparing them. (And nor could football fans. When *Auf pet* had become a massive hit Dick Clement and Ian La Frenais went to see Liverpool play Newcastle at St James' Park. At one point the home fans started singing, 'We all agree, that Oz is better than Yosser.' Clement knew instantly that the series had struck a chord.)

'*Boys from the Blackstuff* was sensational stuff. People compared the two, though in my view there was room for both. I thought the story of Yosser Hughes was the most devastating thing I had ever seen on television and I still think that. It was fantastic. But Alan's characters were in despair, drowning. Ours had taken action and got out, so they were swimming, albeit with some difficulty. I'm not saying it was better, just different.'

It was in the long shadow cast by *Blackstuff* that *Auf pet* appeared on Friday 11 November 1983 at 9 p.m. Kevin Whately recalls being told the transmission time shortly before they finished shooting the series and the appalled reaction it drew from Jimmy Nail. 'Friday night? That's my mates fucked then. Nae bugger's gan to see it!' he complained in true Oz fashion. A few other cast members had a similar view, as did the director, Bamford.

'I thought it was a terrible time. Martin told me and I said, "What do you mean, Friday night? This is about brickies, about lads, and they all go to the pub on Friday night." I thought that was the worst thing that could've happened to it. Happily I was wrong.'

Perhaps Bamford's view of the time was shared by Central as there was no fanfare to launch the series, a surprise considering the pedigree of its writers. Whately feels many people at Central thought they had a turkey on their hands, and were not willing to waste money on its promotion.

'On the way to Germany for the first series, the *TV Times* sent a reporter to do a big feature for the show. She said it was going to be the front page and then six pages inside launching the show. When it appeared, it was only a single column and a picture of me getting my haircut. That was it. Two years later the same lass came out to Spain when we were filming the second series to do another piece. I asked her what had happened to the first one she had done. She said the *TV Times* had been told, "Pull it. It's a total turkey. We want it to die quietly." This had come, so she said, from someone at Central. All the publicity was stalled; they wanted it to be stillborn.'

Fortunately the opposite happened. The programme was a gamble; there was no star to carry it and the main members of the cast were unknowns. The series was about the downwardly mobile at a time when people were being encouraged to move upwards. The production values were low, the soundtrack was barely audible and most scenes were set in a grim prefrabricated hut or a brown, starkly furnished bar.

Facing page: Jimmy Nail, who auditioned as an extra and ended up being offered the part of Oz.

Right: Neville waits forlornly for a train at Düsseldorf.

Below: The lads minus Bomber pose for a publicity shot in Hamburg.

Above: Dennis enjoys a moment's respite from babysitting the rest of the seven.

Right: Barry and Wayne set out to disturb Dennis's peace.

Above: Nail, Holton and Whately at large in the German countryside.

Right: A well-refreshed Jimmy Nail mugs for the camera with guest star Michael Elphick.

The Geordie trio review the day's 'rushes'.

'Gary Holton to wardrobe, Gary Holton to wardrobe.'

It was as far removed from the shoulder pads and swimming pools of *Dallas* and *Dynasty*, other popular shows of the time, as it was possible to be. On the one hand there was Jimmy Nail's broken nose and grey underpants; Chris Fairbank's pockmarked face; Tim Spall's skintight jeans; Kevin Whately's purple T-shirt; Tim Healy's receding hairline; Gary Holton's mullet; and Dave Mackay's pub rock blaring away in the background. On the other there was JR's ten-gallon hat; Dex Dexter's perfect profile; Blake Carrington's silver hair and perma-tan; Alexis Colby's mile-wide shoulder pads; and characters being sucked up by alien spaceships or reincarnated in the shower. The only similarities were Sue Ellen's and Oz's fondness for a tipple.

Yet despite, or even because of these differences, it was obvious from the time that the camera first fell on Oz, Neville and Dennis staring out to sea aboard a ferry to Holland, and Joe Fagin's croaking voice was heard crooning the start of 'Breaking Away', that the show would work. It looked grimly authentic for a start, and the characters were real Geordies. Television viewers were often made to suffer a pale imitation of RADA-trained luvvies doing to the Geordie dialect what Mrs Thatcher was doing to working-class Britain. But there was no denying the authenticity of Oz in particular. As soon as he opened that battered mouth of his a star was born, and the southern half of England was left wishing for subtitles. Nail's performance is raw, but that just means he presents his character in all its surly, ball-scratching glory. His timing is impeccable and the vast majority of the first show's best lines fall to him, all delivered with scabrous contempt. On driving on the right: 'One thing about being near the kerb is you can throw your rubbish right into the ditches without hitting anybody.' On being told the others are discussing the meaning of life: 'Oh yeah, I give that a lot of thought, like, being a bricklayer.' And best of all, after returning to the hut following a bawdy night at a brothel, delivered with a wistful look on his face: 'What was she like? All I can tell you is that sex is in its infancy in Gateshead.'

All the traits of the main characters are conveyed immediately in that first episode (apart from Moxey, who doesn't appear with his dartboard until the second). Neville, the acme of working-class drippiness next to Oz's relentless yobbery, is seen writing postcards to his beloved Brenda from every stop along the way, and often in transit too ('Well here we are in Holland. Oops we went over a bump. Which is strange because Holland is so flat.'). Dennis swiftly emerges as the only voice of sanity. Tim Spall's dithering, pedantic Barry makes a memorable appearance and then returns towards the end, as does Gary Holton's swaggering Wayne – who immediately earns the nickname 'London' and Oz's enmity simply for being born in the Big Smoke ('Spurs. I can tell.'). Then there is Pat Roach, who had finally mastered the West Country accent after his travails at the audition. 'Do you speak English?' Dennis asks him in the shouting, condescending voice all Englishmen use when they are trying to make themselves understood to a foreigner. 'Tis moi mother tongue moi dear,' Bomber replies affably in a cider-soaked voice. The audience knows immediately that, despite their obvious flaws, here are people they know, people they will like.

Once the lads make it to Düsseldorf the real star of the show makes its appearance: the hut. Its grim, brown, wooden walls, rickety steel beds, and rusting lockers plastered with porn conjure up an atmosphere so realistic you can almost smell the sweaty socks and rotting milk. If the best

TV comedy is about anything, then it seems to be about captivity. Whether it be Hancock trapped by the limits of his knowledge and intelligence; Harold Steptoe trapped by his dad and his own wish to be free; Alf Garnett sentenced to living with his wife and vice versa; David Brent cracking weak jokes to an unimpressed workforce in an airless office in Slough. The characters in *Auffet* acknowledge the claustrophobia of their surroundings. ('We'll start tunnelling tonight,' says Oz, surveying the inside of the hut. 'The problem's going to be the dogs and the false papers and the civvy clothes.')

Unlike many first episdoes it does not suffer from too much exposition with the writers taking an age to introduce each character, their traits and their backgrounds. Instead, it gets stuck straight into the main story and relies on the occasional flashback to fill in the gaps. Within the first few minutes you are aware of who everyone is and why they are there, a testament to the skill of Clement and La Frenais. Very few scenes or lines are wasted. Though the name of the band playing dodgy cover versions in the German *bierkeller*, and why they were picked, is anyone's guess. The singer is so flat she makes the walls jealous.

The obvious camaraderie between the actors, and the fun they had making the show, are evident. The interplay between the characters is never stilted; if it had been, the fluidity and wit of the writers' dialogue would have been squandered. Instead it is often inspired. Neville: 'When I came here I had a porpos.' Oz: 'A porpos? I thought yer had a wife, man. What do yer feed it on?'

The critical reaction in the following day's press was, on the whole, positive. The *Daily Mirror* led the hosannas; its critic, Kenneth Hughes, was prescient in reckoning that Jimmy Nail could be a find. 'We can expect to see his ugly mug around for a long time,' he wrote. 'From the minute the boys crossed the German border in Oz's broken-down old banger, singing a ribald version of Rule Britannia, it was all a sheer delight.'

In the following day's *Sunday People* Nina Myskow, the hatchet-faced TV critic who forged a reputation insulting overweight pub singers on TV talent shows during the 1980s, also pronounced the show a hit, though she couldn't resist a couple of excruciating puns. 'I don't know bitter from *bitte*, but I do know what I like,' she wrote in her introduction. 'And I do LOVE *Auf Wiedersehen, Pet*, the new series from Central.' 'A hit? Likely, lads,' was how the piece closed. Nancy Banks Smith in the *Guardian* was another fan, revelling in the richness of the Geordie dialect. She pronounced *Auffet* 'well worth watching'.

It is good to know some things never change, and it cheers the heart to see Mary Kenny of the *Daily Mail* praise the show but complain about the vulgarity of the language used. Twenty years have passed and she is still penning similar pieces for the same paper. Her review is unintentionally hilarious.

'I realise that it is difficult to write a story about three rather gormless working lads from Newcastle going off to be migrant chippies and brickies in Germany without indicating a certain roughness of dialogue,' she tut-tuts from behind her net curtains, 'but the art of the writer is to be able to communicate atmospheres and relationships in a way that shows imagination.'

'I'm sorry to be curmudgeonly,' Mary adds, not sounding very sorry at all, 'but there are some things that need saying over and over again and this is one of them: coarse language on television is offensive to most people, including people who might speak like that themselves.'

To which one might reply, in true Oz style: 'Bollocks!'

Her quibble about the language aside, Mary found much to like about the first episode. Bomber mainly. 'There's one poor great Englishman who keeps saving up £900 and keeps blowing the lot gambling,' she writes, and one half expects her to ask us to kneel down and pray for the saving of his mortal soul. She will not have enjoyed Hugo Williams's review in the left-wing weekly, the *New Statesman*, which praised the show for its grit and authenticity and described the programme as 'excellent'.

The only true dissenting voice was Michael Church in *The Times*. He believed the writing to be accomplished and convincing, the characters to be well conceived and their world to be well perceived. This, however, was not enough: 'According to its producer the show is to a certain extent about the insularity of the British abroad and is heavy with overtones about unemployment. Yes, and yes again. But it is also heavy with something else: an indulgent, mawkish, inverted sentimentality. Auf weidersehen [sic], pets.' Despite his misspelling of wiedersehen, Church's was a valid point: occasionally the show veered towards a misty-eyed view of the working man. Yet it rarely crossed the boundary into outright sentimentality and when it did, it managed to haul itself back. For example, in Episode 10, when Dennis and Neville encounter the dying, misanthropic Hedley and decide to do all they can to help him contact his family, the programme started to develop an unintentionally sickly taste; however, this is swiftly erased by Oz's scheme to smuggle hardcore porn back to England in the old man's coffin. In fact, Oz's existence was a reminder that not all northern working-class males were as stoic and decent as the likes of Dennis. Dick Clement says he and La Frenais wrote the character as a criticism of a certain type of feckless, irresponsible man.

'We really did not approve of Oz. We really tried to write him as a person that it was impossible to approve of. He behaved appallingly to his wife and son, never sent them any money. His attitude to the Germans was terrible. He was politically incorrect before the phrase was even invented. But what happened? People started to like him, and once we met Jimmy we started to like him too. Then in a way he got softened a bit. Maybe we were seduced away from our original intentions.'

The second episode introduced Moxey and has a memorable incident with an unexploded World War Two bomb, which triggers from Oz an outpouring of anti-German feeling unmatched until the front page of The *Daily Mirror* during Euro '96. Episode 3 contains a glaring error. Oz, Neville and Dennis decide to go and watch Sunderland playing in Europe even though, as we learn later in the series, they are all fervent Newcastle United fans. As any casual observer of the intense rivalry between Sunderland and Newcastle United fans can tell you, neither set of supporters would cross the road, never mind mainland Europe, to support the other. The idea of Sunderland playing in Europe is also preposterous. 'Banged to rights,' Clement admits. 'I think we wrote that before we'd decided they were Newcastle fans and we forgot to change it.' It did prove a useful vehicle for Oz to return home to meet his wife Marjorie, whose garish appearance and screeching voice give some indication as to why Oz had departed for Germany so abruptly.

The public's adoration of Oz and the rest of the crew was not immediate, despite *Auf pet*'s reception by the press. However, it is time to dispel a myth that has grown up around the show: namely, that no one watched it at first and then after a few weeks it went stratospheric. The British Audience Research Board (BARB) figures tell a different story. On its opening night the programme was lucky to be part of a strong ITV line-up. *Family Fortunes* at 7 p.m. got 13,586,000 viewers, amd was followed by *The A-Team* at 7.30, which drew 14,089,000. Judi Dench and Michael Williams's wonderful comedy, *A Fine Romance*, drew 13,337,000 viewers in its 8.30 slot. Against the BBC's *Nine O' Clock News* and the dire *Dallas* spin-off, *Knot's Landing*, *Auf pet* managed a creditable 10,806,000 viewers and a 21 per cent share of the total viewing audience. Further analysis of the figures reveals that the show, not unexpectedly, was more popular in the North. Only 14 per cent of BARB's audience panel in the South watched it, compared to 25 per cent in the northeast of England.

A week later *Auf pet* shed almost a million viewers, getting 9,172,000, though whether this was because of disappointment with the first episode or the attraction of ice skating on BBC2 is not known. What is known is that by the next week the audience was back to just over the 10 million mark, while Episode 4 pulled in 9,570,000 on 2 December. On the ninth it rose to only 9,621,000 and there were increasing signs that 9,500,000 would be its average figure – not too spectacular given the time slot and the huge audience it was inheriting from *A Fine Romance*. It is at this point that doubts surfaced about the show. Dick Clement believes the programme would have been pulled there and then had it been screened today.

'Ian and I wrote a series called *Full Stretch* which was aired in the early 1990s, and we were very fond of it. We wrote six and they pulled the plug on it because it wasn't getting the audience they thought it should and they weren't prepared to let it build. *Auf Wiedersehen, Pet* was different; it was allowed to build.'

Clement is mistaken. The show would not have been pulled – it would never have been made. That 13 episodes were commissioned meant it had the time to recruit an audience. Today, the maximum number commissioning editors would risk is six. With an eye on the tabloids, they would not be able to resist casting Ross Kemp or Martin Kemp or Robson Green in the one of the principal roles, thus turning the series into a star vehicle rather than the ensemble piece that so contributed to *Auf pet*'s eventual success.

Roger Bamford says it was around the time when Episode 5 was being screened that executives at Central expressed disquiet about the show, claiming that no one could understand the three main characters' thick Geordie accents. They thought it would never gain popularity, and there were putative discussions about moving it to a later time slot, such as 11 p.m.

'They said, "No one can tell what anyone is saying," and Disgusted of Tunbridge Wells was writing in to say, "Who are these people and why are they speaking like that?" There was a definite move to put it back to a later time. But just as they were considering doing that, after about the third or fourth week, someone noticed the figures were starting to rise so the move was put on hold. Then when it became a hit, of course, it was quickly forgotten that anyone had said anything about the accents or moving the show. But it was deeply concerning for a while. I thought, "Well, that's the end of my career."'

The sixth episode marked the turn. On 16 December 10,900,000 viewers watched Neville being mistakenly accused of raping a German girl. By this time the characters were established, and the audience were beginning to have their favourites. The overwhelming majority went for Oz, on the basis that he had the best one-liners and was the sort of guy who said what he liked and liked what he said. One cannot really imagine anyone citing Neville as the gang member they liked best, but there were a fair few who identified with him. Kevin Whately certainly enjoys playing him.

'There's a side to Neville I really like. It's tiresome, but it's the side that says, "No, this isn't the right thing to do." I've got a mate who's like that. Neville always tries to do the right thing and doesn't like things being unjust. While he's not the sexiest of characters – he's quite henpecked – I'm amazed at the amount of men that have come up to me, who have done National Service or been to Germany, and said, "I was just like Neville." I can empathize with him. Nothing he's ever done has jarred with me.'

Pat Roach sees Bomber as the backbone of the crew. Even though, in that first series, he was prone to blowing his wages on gambling or at the brothel, he was there to help the others out should they find themselves in trouble.

'Bomber was much more experienced than the others. He'd five children for a start, and he had a firm hand. He was probably the only one who could tell people like Oz to shut up and sit down, and get him to listen. There is a finality to what he says, like in the third series when he says, "Dennis is the gaffer; we'll do what he says." He's never got a lot to say but he's good character.'

Timothy Spall turned in a bravado performance as Barry the boring Brummie. The monotonous voice; the way he often takes to answering his own statements in the first series, probably used to years of people ignoring him; the lower-middle-class air that differentiates him from the others, coupled with his innocence and naivety, all stemmed from Spall's immense acting ability. The best parts of his character lay in the detail: as a stalwart of the West Bromwich and District Methodist Table Tennis League; his fondness for herb gardens; and his desire to seek democratic consensus, or at least ask Dennis to seek it. Spall managed to turn what could have been a minor character into a true star of the piece.

Gary Holton's Wayne was a lovable stereotype – the chirpy, charming Cockney who likes to preen himself and brag about his womanising. Holton's gregariousness, self-confidence and palpable love of having a good time all come through in his performance. His interplay with Oz is one of the highlights of that first series, as is the time his character decides to try and tutor Barry, almost certainly still a virgin, in the ways of women with predictably hilarious consequences.

Moxey, the amiable Scouser, may have been the most underwritten role but that did not stop Chris Fairbank developing a whole history for the character.

'From what Dick and Ian had turned him into, I made up a life for him. He has a sister from whom he was separated when they were fostered, and that was bad for him because she was his rock. Which is why he sees the rest of the guys as his surrogate family and being with them is where he finally feels he has a little niche and is accepted for all his quirks and oddities. He would lay down his life for the other guys and this gives him a sense of belonging.'

He admits that when he first learned Moxey was an arsonist he had a problem with it.

'It gave me a problem because, let's face it, it's a bloody serious offence and not that funny. There had to be some kind of mitigating circumstances which allowed the legal system to treat him leniently, and the audience found credible. There had to be something in his character which offset it. It could be that he'd had this terrible life and was getting rid of some internal angst when he set fire to a nightwatchman's hut. It was all to do with loneliness and him being a misfit, rather than psychotic. Which isn't funny.'

At the centre of these disparate characters – the voice of sanity among the madness, the decent working man surrounded by a bunch of overgrown children – was Tim Healy's Dennis. Healy's performance as the traditional grafter who finds himself on his uppers, his marriage disintegrating and his business gone bust, and is then landed with wet-nursing a group of bickering men, is one of the least heralded reasons for the show's success. Without him, the gang's anchor, not only would the group disintegrate but the series would not have been the triumph it was. The exasperated look on his face when he and Dagmar finally find solace in the hotel, only for Wayne and Barry to keep interrupting them, was the look of a man who cannot believe his life has taken this turn

After grabbing almost 11 million viewers, and halfway through its run, *Auf pet* disappeared for a week during the Christmas season. It returned on the last Friday of 1983, on 30 January, and the fact that everyone was sick and tired of watching television over the Christmas period might have contributed to a disappointing audience of 9,170,000. However, the blip was only temporary – on 6 January 1984 the audience was back to 10,295,000. Then, the next week, Friday 13 January, came evidence that *Auf pet* was finally a hit. A staggering 11,513,000 people tuned in to see Michael Elphick's thuggish McGowan disturb the hut's equilibrium. The next week the figure rose to 11,949 million, and the proportion of BARB's panel in the south who watched the show had increased to 17 per cent.

Auf pet was beyond the stage of being merely a hit; it was becoming the most talked about programme on television. In the northeast, pub landlords despised it. Video recorders were not the ubiquitous items they are now, so at nine o'clock on a Friday evening normally crowded pubs were deserted. Everyone was at home watching the latest instalment about 'the lads'. An hour or so later the pubs would fill again. Tim Healy says he had dinner with the managing director of Scottish and Newcastle Breweries, who told him that during *Auf pet's* run beer sales in Newcastle pubs dropped, while sales of cans increased dramatically as people bought carry-outs.

In turn, the show's popularity aroused the interest of the tabloid press, beginning a relationship between programme and press that would eventually culminate in tragedy. At this point the publicity was welcome; *Auffet* appealed to working-class viewers, so coverage in working-class newspapers such as the *Sun* and the *Daily Mirror* was excellent promotion. The *Sun* started it with an 'exclusive' about 'Telly's Wild Bunch.' The piece by Charles Catchpole was no more than a rehash of the press release Central Television had sent out on the eve of the first episode. It had been ignored, but now that the show was a hit the stories about the police being called to the hotel in Hamburg, hookers turning out to be men and squaddies getting drunk were reheated and served under the auspices of the cast being the 'wrecking crew of telly'. The piece claimed that all the mishaps it described had occurred in Germany – even Chris Fairbank breaking his leg, which actually happened in Tooting. But it was all harmless fun. It was the final paragraph that contained the most important news for the programme's legion of fans: 'The show's producers are now planning a second series – set in Spain.'

Further proof of *Auffet*'s burgeoning popularity came when Dave Mackay's theme tune, 'That's Livin' Alright', sung by the gravel-voiced Joe Fagin, reached the UK's Top 10 in January 1984. It was the sound of the opening guitar riff blaring out of his car radio that first alerted Chris Fairbank to the fact that the show he'd believed would sink without a trace had instead become a colossal success.

'The announcer on Capital Radio said, "number four!" Then the song started. "Working on the site from morning 'til night …" I nearly crashed the car. I knew then that it was big; I never thought that would happen, though I've never been happier to be proved wrong.'

Sadly, the viewing figures for Episodes 11 and 12 are missing from the archives. However, we can assume that the upward trend continued because 13,410,000 viewers watched as the series drew to its close on 10 February, tuning in to see the lads return to England, Oz with four pints of German blood swilling around in his veins – though he believed it had come from Neville. It gained a 26 per cent share of the viewing audience; and 21 per cent of BARB's southern panel had been lured away from their shandies to watch it. It was a hit in every sense.

The series' end precipitated a series of valedictory reviews in the newspapers, summed up by Anthea Hall's *Sunday Telegraph* farewell.

'This exceptional series, in the very best traditions of British comedy, has gradually gained the audience it deserves (they're even watching it in Whitehall …). In fact the adventures of a group of brickies in Dusseldorf has developed into a subtle study of a section of humanity, with absolute authenticity of character, not just for a couple (as in Arthur and Terry in *Minder*) but for seven interacting and distinct types.'

Hall ended by pleading for a second series, a view echoed by the *Daily Mirror*'s Hilary Kingsley in a paean to Barry, whom she named as her favourite character thanks to the 'joyous' acting of Tim Spall. It being the *Mirror*, she couldn't resist one last Teutonic pun, however.

'Central TV have pledged some of the lads will be back in more episodes soon. Barry had better be one.

'Or there'll be donner and blitzen from me.'

Dissenting voices remained, mainly in the shape of Sean Day-Lewis of *The Daily Telegraph*, who was slowly becoming the show's *bête noire*. In an earlier review he'd dismissed it by pedantically pointing out that events had already overtaken the basis for the series; namely, that rising unemployment in West Germany had provoked the government into closing the loophole that allowed itinerant workers to be untaxed. The fact that this development was addressed in the final episode did not make him repent. Instead he damned the show with faint praise.

'Admirers place it in the television pantheon somewhere between *The Likely Lads* by the same authors and Alan Bleasdale's *Boys from the Blackstuff*. As an intermittent follower it has seemed to me to lack the character depth of the former and the cutting edge of the latter but it has unarguably been in a likeability class of its own amid the current crop of comedy.'

Day-Lewis did point out that with the hut burned to the ground, and all the characters except Wayne back in England, it would test the ingenuity of the creators to concoct a credible second series. 'Perhaps Oz and company could be reassembled as visiting workers in some other country,' he ended his review.

Now there was an idea.

Above and overleaf: Filming on the ferry on the way back to England.

06: PAST THE POINT OF NO RETURN

For Dick Clement and Ian La Frenais the success of *Auf pet* was immensely gratifying. Moving to Los Angeles had caused some resentment from the British press – a classic case of 'build 'em up, knock 'em down' coupled with accusations that the pair had turned their backs on Britain. To have such a hit silenced the critics, according to La Frenais.

'I remember when it got the cover of *Time Out*. I still have the picture of Tim, Gary and Jimmy. For them, for this trendy London magazine to carry this rave review was amazing. And for Dick and I, who had moved to LA, it felt as if we'd got back our street cred in England. We thought, "We can go back to England now. They're not calling us wankers with swimming pools." Even though we didn't have swimming pools. We were plain old wankers in the sun.'

Clement found the show's popularity even sweeter because it had been the pair's first attempt at a drama series.

'Listen, success is always wonderful. It beats the shit out of the other. We wrote *The Likely Lads*, and, when you're young and foolish, you think, "Oh boy, that's all we have to do. Churn it out and people are going to jump up and down." Then you write a couple of things where that doesn't happen and you learn humility. So I'm always thrilled when people like what we do.'

As the first series finished the pair travelled over to England to talk about a second one which, given the popularity of the first, was a given. La Frenais took the chance to watch his team, Newcastle United, at St James's Park with Tim Healy and Jimmy Nail. He was genuinely taken aback to see what a phenomenon the show was in that part of the world. Many people there believed it had helped to revive a city that had previously been known only for coal, brown ale, grimy buildings, a fading football team that still harked back to a day when its best players were called Len and Malcolm, soaring unemployment and silly accents. The three were given free drink and food in a director's box, and after the game they were taken to meet the Newcastle players, including Kevin Keegan, in the changing room.

All the cast have their own theories as to why the show had the impact it did. Unanimously, they cite the wonderful scripts they worked with. Tim Healy believes it was because *Auf pet* was a genuine working-class programme.

'It was real. I had builders coming up to me and the best compliment you could have is when a bricklayer comes over and says, "I love that show". If an actor comes over and says that, it doesn't really matter. When the people who you are playing are fans, well, that's a great accolade. When they say, "I'm a plasterer…", "I'm an electrician…", or "I worked in Germany", and they loved it, you know you've got it right. "We had a guy just like Oz", they'd say. Every building site has a guy like Oz. Every pub does, for that matter.'

Roger Bamford cites the quality of the writing and thinks that the decision to cast unknowns was influential.

'I don't want to blow my own trumpet, but the way it was cast and the way it was shot certainly contributed. Had it been done conventionally then it might not have worked. I had been brought up by the BBC and was into gritty realism, and I thought comedy works best if you make it real. I could also have cast a conventional character as Oz and he would have been very good, but it wouldn't have had the same impact. I don't know what it was that made me cast Jimmy; I just knew there was something there.'

Franc Roddam's belief is that most people involved in the production – the actors and writers in particular – shared a similar world view.

'The core group, those actors, all believe in the dignity of the working man. Now that may sound like a cliché, but the working men are the majority in this country and sometimes they are set up to be laughed at.

'These are the guys, though, who earn the country its money, who fight its wars, who make things happen. Yet they seem to have a minor voice. Jimmy, Kevin, Tim Healy, Tim Spall, Chris; all of them, in a broad sense, they are political. Pat Roach is less political but he has an incredible sense of decency. That's what makes *Auf Wiedersehen, Pet* remarkable; it takes the mickey out of the working man, but it's sympathetic and in many ways it protects their reputation. That's the key to its success.'

Kevin Whately thinks the chemistry created on set by Roger Bamford was one of the significant reasons for the show's popularity, while Pat Roach believes the quality of the acting was key.

'They are wonderful, wonderful actors, all of them. I learned from them as I went along, just by watching them all. Wherever I am at this stage I owe to them. Because they were so good, and the scripts were so good, it made for a brilliant formula.'

Julia Tobin has no hesitation in saying who the catalysts were.

'We knew the show was funny but we didn't know it would get so many viewers. It is all down to Dick and Ian. The guys are brilliant, all seven of them worked very hard during that first series, we all did, and they deserve every accolade they get. But it is all down to the writing. Dick and Ian are so good at comedy, yet they are also able to incorporate fantastic drama.'

Even Noel Clarke, who was cast to play Wyman, Wayne's son, in the third series has a theory – and he was in short trousers when the first series was shown.

'*Auf Wiedersehen, Pet* was every working man's dream, wasn't it? Blokes wanted to be part of that gang. To be in Germany with your mates, having a laugh; what could possibly be better than that? When my mate's dads found out I was going to be in it, they loved it because it was their favourite programme. In the pub they'd be telling everyone, "I've known this boy since he was this high," and all that stuff.'

Whatever the reasons behind the show's success, the stark fact was that the lives of its cast were irreparably changed for ever. This took them by surprise. From being unknown outside their own sitting rooms the principal members became public property, unable to nip out for a quick pint or go to the shops. Particularly in Newcastle. And particularly if you happened to be Jimmy Nail. He had a difficult time adjusting to his new-found notoriety. Chris Fairbank recalls that just prior to the end of filming, Nail had been looking forward to going back to his old job and seeing his mates.

'He was always telling these fabulous stories about the people he worked with. "That's what I'll be doing as soon as I finish this," he kept saying. "I'll be back in my job." What he really wanted to do was to get his music happening. But his success was overnight. One week he was watching the programme and when it finished he went down to his local for a beer, and the next thing he knew he was being mobbed and chased down the street.'

Pat Roach recounts how Nail turned up to watch him wrestle in Croydon town hall between the show being filmed and screened. He took a seat in the front row. 'In a few weeks time, you won't be able to sit there,' Roach told him. 'Aah, haddaway,' Nail replied. Roach was right though; Nail's instantly recognizable face, the same face that had earned him the part of Oz in the first place, was to become a curse because there was never any doubt that it was 'him off the telly'. Worst of all, according to Healy, people thought Nail was like his screen character.

'It was so difficult for Jimmy. Oz is a brilliant character; however, for the world to think you are that person is horrible. It's not so bad if you're Dennis. People think you are sensible. Though, having said that, they think you're approachable, so early on when I went out with Jimmy people would come up to me. They were too frightened to talk to him and wanted me to introduce them! And for Jimmy, being such a big guy, well, he got noticed whenever he walked into a pub. I was all right; I could hide behind people. I wouldn't be noticed. When you're Jimmy's size, and famous too, people see you straight away, then you get idiots coming over and it got very tough for him.'

Nail was not the only one to become a local hero. Healy remembers walking into Marks & Spencer in Newcastle to buy a pair of trousers, and before he knew it the store manager was at his arm, welcoming him warmly, offering to take him around the shop. Eventually, after going into the staff canteen and shaking hands and smiling at everyone for an hour, he managed to extricate himself.

For Whately, Healy and Nail, the zenith of their fame came when they decided to attend a concert by Billy Connolly at Newcastle city hall. As they walked through the door they were spotted instantly and surrounded. Whately, only half in jest, compares it to being a member of the Beatles.

'We'd barely got in the door and we were mobbed. It was quite frightening because we were crushed in a corner and no one would move in any direction. Billy couldn't get his show started because of the crush so they had to send over stage crews and bouncers to drag us out. We knew Billy, so we went and watched it from backstage and they sneaked us out of the stage door just before the end. It was strange and really affected us all. It was the first time I really thought, "Bloody hell, this is big."'

The unreality of being transformed from obscure actors to household names and faces brought the cast closer together. Births and parties meant they saw each other socially, often shaking their heads over a beer at how weird it was to become the focus of tabloid interest. Most of them are private men, wary of the limelight and fiercely protective of their and their family's privacy. The only exception was Gary Holton, as one would expect of the singer in a rock band. He loved the attention, and was comfortable fielding the calls of, and befriending, journalists or being seen out and about in London.

'He took it in his stride. He always had time to speak to people and sign autographs. He wasn't the sort to play the prima donna and the fame never went to his head. He was always just Gary.'

From being jobbing actors constantly in search of roles, the cast were in demand. Knowing a second series was a certainty, most of them found interim work. Tim Healy appeared in an episode of *Minder*; Whately got a role in *Miss Marple*; Spall, in an indication of things to come, bagged a role in *The Bride*, a remake of *The Bride of Frankenstein* (directed by Franc Roddam); Nail did *Minder* and got his much sought-after music career off the ground, doing a deal with Virgin Records that would yield a hit single in the summer of 1985 – a version of Rose Royce's 'Love Don't Live Here Anymore'. It went to number three in the charts (the same position, coincidentally, as 'That's Livin' Alright' reached) and earned him a rather nervous appearance on *Top of the Pops*; Roach continued his movie career, starring alongside Arnold Schwarzenegger

Right: Gary Holton toasts the success of the first series ...

in *Conan the Destroyer*, as well as doing a *Minder*; Fairbank got a bit part in David Hare's film *Plenty* and also landed a role in a play at the Royal Court in London; Holton, meanwhile, starred in the West End musical *Pump Boys and Dinettes* and, somewhat inevitably, appeared in *Minder*.

Halfway through the screening of the first series Clement and La Frenais had been asked to start planning a second one. The big question, of course, was where? They knew the success and humour of the first series had come from the 'fish out of water' syndrome; from having the group cast adrift in a foreign culture. The hunt was on for a suitable place for them to wash up in for series two. La Frenais says they never considered sending them back to Germany.

'Perhaps it was a stupid idea to burn the hut down and not to keep them in Germany. It would have been a better idea with hindsight. But you don't think of these things at the time. We liked the idea of "Now they go somewhere else."'

Once the pair had the central idea of the lads getting involved with a local gangster, sending them to Spain suggested itself. In the mid-1980s parts of the southern Spain coastline, the so-called Costa del Crime, was home to a number of British villains in 'hiding'. A 100-year-old extradition treaty between Britain and Spain had ended in 1978 and wasn't replaced until 1985, making the area a bolt hole for the likes of Ronnie Knight and Freddie Foreman, both of whom eventually came back to England to do their time.

For research, Bamford, Clement and La Frenais, and Stan Hey, whose services had been retained, travelled to Marbella for five days in February 1985. They found exactly what they wanted, in particular in a bar called The Office, which was a home from home for every shady character in the area, as La Frenais recollects.

'We went in there one night. There were all these really dodgy guys in there, people like Ronnie Knight. They all looked us, then they started asking us, "Who are you?" We explained we were writers and one of us mentioned that we wrote *Porridge*. Of course, from that point on they started buying us drinks. In the middle of the bar was a phoney gold ingot, as a tribute to the Brinks Mat robbery or something. We went back there on a Sunday lunch time, when all their wives were with them, done up to the nines. They were having a sing-song and it was just desperate. They were all there together, not a Spaniard in sight, singing Neil Diamond songs, trying to convince themselves that this was the life they'd always dreamed of leading. I'll never forget that trip.'

Hey has a hazy recollection of trying to befriend the locals.

'I'd had a few beers and I asked Ronnie Knight if he'd let me buy him lunch. He said, "No thanks." I had no idea what I was thinking of. The next morning I woke up in a cold sweat, thinking, "What if he'd said yes?" But it was good research and we got some good material. The problem was how we were going to get the lads out to Spain.'

Hey says Saudi Arabia and the Falklands were other options for the series, but the first was a place where alcohol was prohibited, and therefore not a natural home for seven thirsty brickies, while the second didn't offer as many possibilities as Spain. Clement, La Frenais and Hey, armed

with all their research, went away to write the next series. Hey remembers that in the hotel in Spain, Clement and La Frenais sat at one end of a lounge with him at the other.

'Dick and Ian would shout every now and again, "Any ideas yet, apprentice?" I'd say. "Not yet. You're not paying me enough." For a couple of days we sketched in the rest of the series, because we couldn't set it all in Spain and we weren't sure how to get it all together again. Eventually it came together and I was given the task of writing three episodes around Thornley Manor and then one out in Spain.'

The show's producers and Bamford then set about persuading the cast to return for another series. In the main this was an easy task, but it was made more expensive by Central's decision, before the series grew huge, not to contract the cast for another series. This might have been because the company didn't anticipate a second series. The success of the first series and the chance to renegotiate granted the actors and their agents the opportunity to extract far more money for a second one. All of them agreed to return. The only potential problem was with Jimmy Nail, whose ascent had been disturbingly rapid and who was already beginning to feel that the character of Oz was a millstone. Chris Fairbank remembers Nail's unenviable dilemma over whether to play Oz and risk further typecasting, or not doing the series and disappointing the show's legion of fans.

'To put it mildly, Jimmy was very worried. He was afraid that he would be misunderstood; that people would apply all Oz's traits to him; that they would believe he was this stereotypically thick bloke from the northeast, which Jimmy certainly isn't. He's very shrewd and sharp. It caused him horrendous problems and for that reason he wasn't too keen on doing anything more with Oz. I did hear that Central were so set on doing a second series that they would've gone ahead without him. Which would have been terrible. The series would have bombed I think. The nation would have gone, "Hang on, where's Oz?"'

The 'will he, won't he' saga made wonderful copy for the press, which attempted to turn Nail into the villain of the piece, painting him as becoming too big for his boots, of wanting more money than the other actors, which wasn't the case. Some members of the cast and crew weren't so sure Nail's reluctance was that genuine; the view was that his agent might simply have been trying to get the best possible deal for his client, and used the press as a bargaining tool. Whatever the reason, by the end of 1984 the issue was finally resolved and preparations began for filming the second series.

The tabloids also enjoyed speculating about both the location and the name of the second series. In the *Sun* Charles Catchpole was under the impression it was to be called *Hasta La Vista, Pet*, but he was correct in saying the location was Spain. In an interview with the *Daily Star* in January 1985, Gary Holton confirmed this and offered more information on the plot. 'We are based in England, but have these business excursions and adventures in Spain,' he told Pat Codd. He promised there would be 'plenty of sun and bottles'.

07: NO ONE SAID IT WAS GOING TO BE EASY

The second series of *Auf Wiedersehen, Pet* went into production in the spring of 1985. Central Television had relocated its studios to Nottingham from London the year before and there was a few months' filming there before the company moved to Spain in the late summer and early autumn. In Nottingham, most of the actors and Roger Bamford stayed at the George rather than having the luxury of driving in from home as they had in London. Bamford remembers the hotel as 'interesting'.

'The first night I was there I got to my room. I decided to have a gin and tonic from the minibar but I realized there was no ice. I phoned reception and asked if they could bring me a bucket of ice. Five minutes later there was a knock on my door and there was this guy with a fire bucket filled to the brim with ice. I thought, "Welcome to Nottingham."'

Shortly after the cameras started rolling the first of several problems that would bedevil the making of the series forced a hasty rewrite from Clement and La Frenais. Caroline Hutchinson, who played Vera, Dennis's soon to be ex-wife, in the first series, was taken ill. According to Julia Tobin she had attended the read-through before the shoot began believing she was suffering from jaundice. It turned out to be cancer for which she would need chemotherapy. Obviously she was unable to take her role in the series, though in a kind gesture the cast all requested that Central fulfil her contract.

The question of how to replace her remained. The thought of casting another actress to fill the role was dismissed out of hand. Instead, the writers chose to split the character in two. Dennis was supposed to have been living at home with Vera, though their marriage wasn't working. Instead, he was shown to be staying with his sister, played by Jimmy Nail's real-life sister, Val McLane. To provide Dennis with love interest, the role of Christine Chadwick was written. The part was given to Kevin Whately's real-life wife, Madelaine Newton who, ironically, had auditioned for the part of Vera for the first series and lost out to Caroline Hutchinson. Just to complicate matters further, Neville and Brenda's daughter was played by Whately and Newton's daughter, Catherine. Whately initially had some doubts about this.

'At first I wasn't too keen for her to be in it. But Martin, the producer, said it would be only two days' studio time and that Madelaine could come out to Spain too when we went to film there. So when Caroline fell ill Madelaine was there on the spot.'

Caroline Hutchinson managed to recover from that bout of cancer – and was able to star in the film *Stormy Monday* alongside Sting in 1988. Tragically, she fell ill once again and died, a loss deeply felt by every single member of the *Auf pet* cast and crew.

Yet another problem facing the programme-makers was a background of industrial unrest within the television industry, and at Central in particular. It was 1985 and the dying days of the strong hold that the EETPU (the electricians' union) had on the industry. They were locked into a dispute with the management at Central over working conditions. At the time there was an unwritten rule, soon to be rewritten, that when the electricians, known as 'sparks' went out on strike other unions would join them. This would cripple Central and for this reason management were very wary of upsetting the sparks, fearing major industrial action. With this knowledge, the electricians were able to retain many of their 'Spanish practices'. Roger Bamford remembers the time well.

'In Nottingham it was a completely different atmosphere than Elstree. They were forming a new company in many ways and we were one of their biggest dramas, so we were picked on. I'll give you one example that has stuck in my mind ever since.

'We were filming on the streets of Nottingham at a house and it started to rain. Suddenly the first assistant came up to me and said, "Sorry, we're going to have to stop filming." I said, "Why? The rain's fine." He said, "No, the electricians are refusing to work because they haven't got any gear and the management wouldn't give them any." So we decided we'd better sort it out. There were phone calls made everywhere, and the management sent a whole lot of wet-weather gear out. So they all got into them and we started filming again. We went on and the rain stopped, and so they all took all their gear off and put it in the back of the van. We went on. Then it started to rain again. The first assistant came up and said, "Sorry, they've stopped working again." I said, "Now what's the problem." He said, "Well, apparently they've taken their gear off and it hasn't been washed, and they refuse to put it back on again until it has been taken away and cleaned." That is how petty it was. The whole of the second series was dogged with that. Any petty argument the management and unions could have they would. It was a dreadful time, completely different to the first series. I have Martin McKeand to thank in many ways because

Right: Caroline Hutchinson in her role as Vera. Sadly, illness prevented her from taking part in series two.

he shielded me from it and dealt with it, so it meant I could try and concentrate on making a programme.'

On location in Nottingham and in Newcastle the actors and crew had to contend with a novel problem: crowds of fans. Once word spread across the Midlands that the new series was being filmed in the area people would turn up to watch, causing untold headaches. Of course, it was even worse in Newcastle. While Tim Spall was being filmed emerging from Newcastle railway station he was mobbed by a crowd of fans, much to his bewilderment. Things got more hysterical at Newcastle airport when the seven turned up to film their departure for Spain, as Chris Fairbank recalls.

'For some reason British Airways had pulled the fleet of planes that usually shuttled people to London and back. They had for a short period of time replaced them with Concorde. So hundreds of people had descended on the airport to see Concorde. This coincided with us lot filming there. This made a lot of people very excited and before we knew what was happening there were crowds everywhere. It was like being a Beatle in 1964. They ushered us to safety behind those doors in an airport where you're never sure what lies behind them.'

Over spring and summer the crew filmed the Thornley Manor section of the series, in particular at Beesthorpe Hall in Caunton which doubled as the country house. It was while filming there that Tim Healy narrowly escaped serious injury, or worse, when he was driven from the hotel to work one morning in Pat Roach's Porsche.

'The bus arrived to take us to work and Pat said, "You want a ride?" There's a long, dead straight road that goes into Thornley Manor, about a mile long. He said, "I'll open it up and let you see what it can do." I didn't have my seat belt on. We were always first to work; there was never anyone coming out. There's a brow, a hump in the drive. We were doing about 75 m.p.h. and we went over the top. As we did, the designer was coming the other way. He saw us flying towards him so he put his brakes on and his foot stuck on the brake pedal. We hit him head-on. Pat slammed the brakes on. I went straight through the windscreen. I went through it, hit my chest on the front dash and went back. Pat braced himself and pushed the steering column into the engine. No one else would have had the strength to do that. He just damaged his back a bit. I hit this thing with my chest and I remember not being able to breathe. The next thing was the ambulance arriving and them saying, "Don't move, you've probably broken a lot of ribs." The guy said to me, "You've moved the dash five inches out of line." I was in hospital for three days and I was really badly bruised, and it took me about three weeks to get over it. I was dead lucky. I got the bus after that. Pat was horrified.'

Then it was time to move out to Spain for a five-week location shoot. Whately and his family went out with Jimmy Nail and his wife Miriam and their son Tommy a day or two before filming was due to start in Marbella. The day after they arrived Whately spoke on the phone to Tim Spall, who had been turned back at the airport. The sparks had called a strike, the crew and cast been sent home and a decision had been taken by Central's management, so Whately remembers, to cancel the whole series.

'He said to me, "They've just turned me back from the airport. They won't let us get on the plane." The series had been cancelled, he said. Everyone had gone back home to refill their fridges with food, get their cats and dogs back out of kennels. I went and found Roger Bamford and Martin McKeand, who were already out there. They were having dinner in the hotel. I told them what Tim had said. Martin phoned Nottingham that evening and came back and said, "It's off." He said we were welcome to have a few days' holiday before flying back. We decided to have a few days. I really thought that was it because the message from the start had been, "If there's any trouble, we'll call the whole thing off."

'We'd become a pawn for the management to beat the unions with. They'd been tempting people to relocate from London to Nottingham with the prospect that the next series of *Auf pet* would be filmed there. They were saying to them, "If you act up, the lads won't come." Meanwhile, the unions were thinking, "They're bluffing. This is their flagship programme, they wouldn't dare pull it." So we were caught in the middle of this power struggle.'

Luckily for everyone concerned, the production was back on track the next day and people were allowed to fly to Spain. It would have been a painful irony if a show that celebrated the working man had been crippled and eventually cancelled as a result of industrial action. Whately is not anti-union, yet he acknowledges that the following eight or nine months didn't go smoothly. Chris Fairbank is more vociferous.

'Both sides, the unions and the management, were using the success of the first series to extract whatever it was they wanted and we got caught in the middle of it. Every day there seemed to be some sort of problem that had to be overcome. During that experience I lost all sympathy for the unions because I experienced how, when union power gets out of hand, it does nothing but destroy everyone else's ability to do the jobs. They were greedy, lazy bastards the lot of them. The job was made virtually impossible.'

Julia Tobin remembers that when filming in Spain got under way at last, the lights would go out at six o'clock without fail, and filming would have to stop because the electricians refused to work for a second longer. This meant the chances of getting the requisite amount of film 'in the can' before the scheduled end of the shoot decreased and everyone had to work doubly hard to compensate.

Not that the actors were able to fill their leisure time lounging by the pool or on the beach. The Spanish section was at the end of the series, and all the studio scenes were to be filmed back in Nottingham. It was imperative that the cast not develop suntans, and so spoil continuity, and they were forbidden to sunbathe. Julia Tobin remembers how they organized day trips and a host of other events to occupy their time on days off, to stop them pining for the beach.

'Central hired an apartment block within a hotel complex where we all stayed. We had trips out, parties, barbecues, a table tennis tournament, which Tim Healy won. He's very good. But it was frustrating because there was all this fantastic, brilliant sunshine and yet we couldn't sunbathe. The crew could, of course, so they were out there all day. They were bronze and we were all pasty white. Apart from Gary Holton. There was no way people were going to keep Gary away from the beach. They just lathered him head to foot in factor 58 suncream.'

Holton was enjoying himself on the shoot in other ways. Due to the show's high profile, journalists turned up in Spain to sate the public's appetite for *Auf pet* stories. Their main target was Holton. According to his manager, John Harwood Bee, former acquaintances were approaching the press with revelations about him using drugs. Holton did have a problem with heroin, and with the support of his agent and Harwood Bee, was in the process of cleaning himself up. The problem had resurfaced during the summer's shooting in Nottingham, leading to an argument between the actor and other members of the production team about his erratic behaviour. As a consequence, Central asked Harwood Bee if he would accompany Holton during the shoot in Spain. The manager agreed.

'Gary had a drug problem for a number of years but we weren't aware of it until about a year or 18 months before he died. His agent and I helped to clean up, and he'd had counselling and was getting cleaner and cleaner. That summer, though, his behaviour was erratic and it started to affect his work, so Central called a meeting and asked if we'd accompany him to Spain. We did, and to my knowledge he was fine.'

Holton would always be Holton, however. Harwood Bee remembers one day of filming which featured a chauffeur-driven Bently. There was a delay before the cameras rolled and Holton had run out of cigarettes, so he commandeered the car complete with driver. 'You couldn't run us into town to get some fags, guv?' he asked. An hour later he still hadn't returned and filming was under way. He was not universally popular on his return.

On a more serious note, stories of Holton's drug problems had reached the tabloids, who were now obsessed with all things *Auf pet*. The *Daily Star* sent a reporter and photographer to speak to him, but everyone on the production had agreed that they wouldn't speak to the press until filming had finished. Harwood Bee told the reporter that when he returned to England he would speak to the *Star* about the possibility of the actor giving them an exclusive once the series had wrapped. He knew people were trying to sell stories about Holton to the press, so the intention was that Holton would admit to his problem and talk about his efforts to rid himself of his addiction, warning people away from drugs in the process. The *Star* seemed satisfied – for the time being at least.

So, in Spain the problem wasn't fans turning up and watching the show being filmed. Instead, it was journalists sniffing around trying to uncover stories for a media that was increasingly interested in the private lives of the programme's main players. Still, the trip was sociable enough. The makers of San Miguel beer, seeing what the success of the first series had done for the sale of Becks, stepped in to provide crates and crates of beer for drinking both on and off set.

Despite the problems with journalists and electricians, most of the cast have fond memories of working in Spain. Shooting culminated with a day at sea filming the final scenes of the series, where Barry and Hazel are married on the boat that is whisking Ally Fraser to Morocco. While the weather was good, Julia Tobin has mixed feelings about the experience.

Below right: Crowds gather in Newcastle city centre to watch filming of the second series.

A scene familiar to all fans of the series — Neville and Brenda in the marital bed.

Behind the scenes during filming in Spain.

Clockwise: The Whately family; guest star Bill Paterson and friends; Melanie Hill and friend; and the Whatelys arrive for filming.

The cast and crew relax in Spain. Roger Bamford (below left) makes an ill-advised foray on to the dance floor.

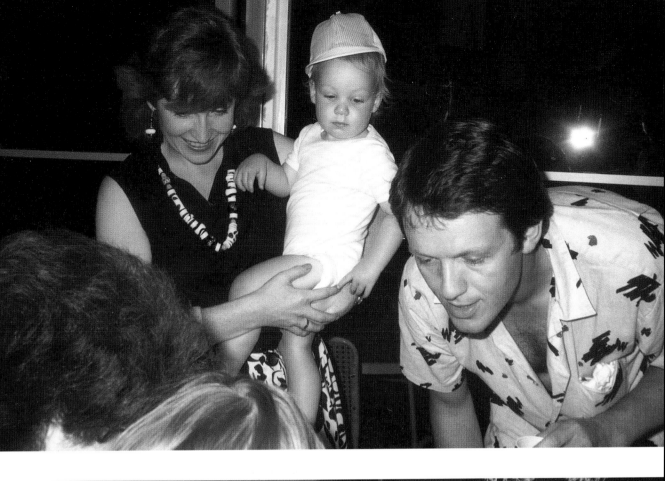

'There was no place to shelter on the boat and we spent all day on it. You couldn't go below deck because the bilge pump stank to high heaven. We were on deck for 12 hours; most people were hanging over the sides. I didn't get seasick, though we were at sea for so long that it took me a while to walk straight, before I got my land legs.'

With all the troubles surrounding the second series, the accidents and the strikes, Chris Fairbank believed the show was becoming ill-fated, as if it wasn't meant to be. But the difficulties only served to bring the cast closer together, to strengthen the bond between them. Unfortunately, a further tragedy was waiting around the corner – one that would bring the group even closer, yet end any immediate prospect of there being a third series of *Aufpet*.

After Spain, shooting continued without further mishap, other than the occasional strike, until it was time to film the interior scenes in the Nottingham studios. On Thursday 25 October filming ended in the early evening and the cast headed back to their homes. They were due to rehearse scenes in Hammersmith in London on the Friday morning and then head back up to Nottingham on Sunday night to resume filming. All the cast arrived for the rehearsal, except for Gary Holton. According to some of the actors this wasn't the first time he had either been late or failed to show. Bamford used the phone in the corridor, and asked Holton's agent where he was before deciding to start the rehearsal with Holton's lines divided among the rest of the cast.

Around mid-morning the phone rang. Bamford went to answer it. It was Holton's agent to say that Holton had been found dead in bed at an address in Wembley earlier that morning.

'I just thought, "We're in the middle of the rehearsal. I just can't go back into that room to tell them." I was in shock I suppose. I went back to the room and was going to get on with the rehearsal. I said, "Right, where were we?" Jimmy, being canny, knew something was wrong. He said, "What was that phone call about?" I thought I couldn't lie, so I said, "His agent has told me that Gary's died." Of course, there was nothing we could do then; it was about 11, so we packed it in and went to one of the pubs on the Thames and had a drink. Our emotions were very mixed.'

Everyone was numb. Holton was 32. He had been acting with them only the day before. Now he was dead. Given his lifestyle, few people expected him to be around to draw his pension, but no one expected him to die. Julia Tobin says he was a 'naughty boy' but no one thought his life was in danger. As they sat waiting for him to arrive that Friday morning, she remembers them cursing his name for leaving them in the lurch. They weren't to know he was dead.

Julia Tobin hadn't been at the rehearsal, and heard the news from her brother. She'd acted with Holton on the Wednesday before returning to London that evening. On the Saturday morning, when the story broke in the press, her brother called her.

'"Shame about Gary," he said. I knew nothing about it because I hadn't seen the newspapers. No one had called me. I said, "What do you mean?" He said, "He's dead." "Don't be ridiculous," I said, "I was only acting with him on Wednesday." He said he'd read about it so I ran to the shop and bought the newspapers. It was such a shock and I didn't know how we were going to carry on. Everyone was immensely depressed by it.'

The extent of Holton's problems with drink and drugs differs according to different members of the *Auf pet* team. Clement and La Frenais knew he had a problem because, given the actor's unreliability, they were often being asked to rewrite scenes to exclude Wayne. According to Clement, Holton had been in bad shape for a while.

'The build-up to him dying was particularly difficult. We had to downplay his character a bit, and the situation had been worrying for some length of time so it didn't come as a total surprise when Martin called me to say he was dead. Saying that, though, no one expected him to die. It was very, very sad.'

Clement's view is echoed by Fairbank. Holton's behaviour had led him to become isolated from the others, he says.

'When he died it was a terrible shock, though not a surprise in some ways. He was living the rock star lifestyle, though those of us that knew him knew it wasn't him really. He became isolated and surrounded himself with people who let him do whatever it was he was doing. Gary did his own thing when he wasn't working, and he wasn't around us much.'

The cast don't deny that Holton's lifestyle directly caused his death. What still rankles with them is the behaviour of the tabloid press, and the indirect part it played in his downfall. To understand the damage the tabloids did it is essential to list what is known, on the record, about Holton's death and the lead-up to it.

In the inquest into his death, held on 19 December 1985, Dr Ninian Marshall told coroner Dr David Paul that Holton had been taking drugs since 1983. He had first come to him for treatment in December 1984. He immediately stopped taking heroin and used a heroin substitute until he completely kicked the habit in March 1985, a few weeks after filming of the second series commenced. However, according to Dr Marshall, Holton suffered a relapse during the summer of 1985 and took heroin every day for a week. This lapse might have explained some of Holton's unreliability during filming. A few weeks later he had managed to give up heroin once more. It was also a matter of record that Holton was a heavy drinker.

In the week preceding his death the press had turned on him. Where once Holton was simply an 'Outrageous TV Star', he was now a 'Heroin Hoodlum'. The turnabout came when a former partner of Holton's sold a story about his lifestyle in which allegations were made about his drug addiction. On 22 October the *Daily Star* ran a piece in which a former agent alleged that he had once had to lock Holton away for a month in an attempt to cure him of his addiction. The drip-drip of revelations merely whetted the appetite of both the *Sun* and the *Star*. Once his friends, both newspapers were now his enemies.

Perhaps understandably, when two *Daily Star* journalists, Neil Wallis and Geoff Baker, and a photographer had tracked him down on to his local pub on the 22nd, Holton had failed to welcome them with open arms and a glass of something bubbly. Instead, he and a friend became involved in an argument with the journalists during which his friend was reported to have broken the photographer's camera and threatened both journalists. Holton and his friend wisely chose to leave but the damage had been done. The next day the *Star* ran the preposterous and irresponsible headline 'Heroin Hoodlum'. There was no indication that Holton was on heroin when the incident took place, or that he was suffering the effects of taking the drug. Nor was he a hoodlum. There was no previous evidence that he was violent. The word 'hoodlum' was used only because a lazy sub-editor needed an alliterative word to go with 'heroin'. The impact on Holton was devastating.

The next day he was understandably upset, a feeling compounded when his mother fell ill after reading the allegations about her son. This in turn depressed Holton who, because of the shooting schedule, was unable to get up to Shropshire to see her. The next day, after filming in Nottingham Kevin Whately and his wife left the studio. As they passed Holton's dressing room they saw him sitting with his head in his hands. Whately remembers.

'He was really depressed. Madelaine went in and put her arm around him and said something about it all being "fish and chip paper" and for him to ignore it. He was upset and he said, "I thought they were my friends," meaning the journalists. We watched him go into a tailspin that week; it all just got to him.'

Whately is still angry about the way his friend was treated by the press, and that he died a broken, unhappy man. So is Tim Healy.

'They called him a "heroin hoodlum" and he came into work with his chin on the floor, and then his mother fell ill. Two days later he was dead, and I'm sure what was in the papers had something to do with it.'

At Holton's funeral all the actors were astounded when the press trampled over graves and wreaths trying to get pictures of the cast. Healy remembers that a writer sat behind them making notes about their reaction during the service. All in all, the nation's tabloids emerge from the whole saga with little credit. Holton was naive in thinking that his relationship with the press was a 'friendship', that it was only one-way. Something like this was bound to happen the more he kept himself in the public eye. Once the press discovered he'd had a problem with heroin it was obvious they were going to publish the fact, regardless of how many stories he'd given them. *Auf pet* was big news; articles about its cast sold newspapers. But that does not excuse the stories that depicted Holton as a 'heroin hoodlum', which was a shameful piece of reporting.

The coroner recorded an open verdict on the basis that there were too many 'unanswered questions' about Holton's death. Levels of morphine and alcohol were found in his blood. After returning to London from Nottingham he had gone to a pub. In the early hours of the morning he had turned up at a friend's house in Wembley where he had a cup of tea before going to bed. No one saw him leave the room before he left it to sleep, no one saw him take a fix of heroin and no syringe or any other material for drug abuse was discovered. As a result, the coroner was unable to say what it was that killed the actor.

John Harwood Bee is adamant about the cause of death: the press.

'The behaviour of the tabloid press, and the *Daily Star* in particular, was absolutely disgusting and despicable. They targeted Gary. He was a strong guy and was able to handle most things, but what they were doing was total destruction. Under the stress of the onslaught by the newspapers I think he simply gave way and returned to some bad habits. It was a tragic end to a very talented life.'

For the rest of the cast there was uncertainty alongside obvious grief. No one knew what Holton's death meant for the future of the series. Many of the studio scenes had yet to be shot, but there was so much film 'in the can' that it was decided that the show could be saved and the character of Wayne would still appear. Clement and La Frenais were called upon to rewrite certain scenes, usually slimming down the number of characters who appeared, to cloak Wayne's absence. Occasionally, they wrote excuses as to why Wayne wasn't with a group when they entered a room after being seen walking down the street with him. The biggest change was the development of the relationship between Oz and Vicky, played by Lesley St John, which was made more prominent.

On the Sunday night following Holton's death, when the cast gathered in the George in Nottingham, the atmosphere was subdued and sombre. That was still the case the next morning as they finished filming a scene they had started with Holton. It's the one at the beginning of Episode 9 where the gang are playing snooker in Newcastle while waiting for the clearance to go to Marbella. Holton had shot the early part of the scene, when the lads banter, but the second part leading up to, and after, Dennis's arrival with news of the trip was yet to be filmed. Tim Healy still remembers how difficult it was.

'It was a couple of days since we'd heard he'd died and we stood there as they played the scene back to us on the monitor so we could see where he was standing. They brought in a double so there was someone there to speak to, and we had to pretend he was there, throwing jokes to him and each other, and all the while we were watching him on the monitor.'

No one felt like continuing. While not everyone got on all the time, the group liken themselves to a family and Holton's loss was similarly felt. The seven actors, and Bamford, had been through a great deal together. According to Fairbank, the atmosphere was terrible until someone cracked a joke and a few people laughed. 'It was if the spirit of the show had returned,' he said. 'Though of course it would never be the same again.

'That was a very difficult day. It was strange to be made to work so soon after, but with hindsight it was probably the best thing that could've happened. We were all devastated but we ploughed on. Had they decided to wait a few weeks before resuming it would have been impossible to get back into it.'

Whately says that, understandably, the gilt had come off the series for the cast. What had been the most enjoyable work in the world had suddenly become a whole lot less fun. Their main aim was not to do the best job possible; it was simply to save the show by finishing the shoot regardless of all the problems. But a feeling was already surfacing among them that the second series would be the last. No one would want to continue without Gary.

The series was saved. Thanks to Clements' and La Frenais' hasty rewrites and some careful editing, Gary Holton's absence was worked around. Only once did a double have to be used on screen, when Wayne attempts to chat up Ally Fraser's girlfriend and is physically lifted out of a casino by Bomber. The man Roach is seen holding above his head was a stand-in, though the shot prior to that is of Holton speaking to Lesley St John. Bamford says there was never any thought of halting production.

'Continuing posed a few problems because in Spain we filmed him going through a door but we hadn't filmed the studio part, so people would notice he isn't there. There were re-writes, people saying, "Where's Wayne?" and once we had to get a double. Because we had a lot of him in Spain it meant we didn't have to drop Wayne from the show and reshoot. For the first two weeks after he died it was very difficult; we just got on the best we could. In sort of a strange way we accepted it, I suppose.'

In January 1986 the filming of the second series of *Auf pet* eventually ended, and for the main members of the cast and crew it could not have come too soon. It was a suitably muted end to a troubled and dispiriting 11 months.

08: THE MAGNIFICENT SEVEN RIDE AGAIN

On 21 February 1986, *Auf Wiedersehen, Pet* returned to British TV screens in its now familiar slot of Friday at 9 p.m. Culturally there was very little happening at the time in Britain; the other talked about television programme of that year was the increasing popularity of an Australian soap opera called *Neighbours*. Meanwhile, the music charts were dominated by big-haired purveyors of power ballads, like Jennifer Rush and Berlin. In current affairs Mrs Thatcher still seemed unassailable. All this might explain why both the viewing public and the critics greeted the return of *Aufpet* with such rapturous delight.

To this viewer at least, watching the second series now, it seems clear that something was lost from the first one. Whether this was down to a bout of 'sequelitis', a consequence of the troubles that had afflicted filming or simply because it wasn't as good as the first series, something seems to be missing. The first episode appears contrived, which in many ways is understandable. For the first series there was a unifying idea: seven men trying to earn a living thrust together. That didn't exist for the second; instead a situation had to be developed in which all the men could be yoked together once more. Therefore the first two episodes deal with the convolutions and plot contrivances of reuniting the lads and lacks the pace and vitality so evident in that first series.

Having said that, *Auf pet* at half-throttle still outclassed most other shows on television at the time.

The first series was exactly that – a series; each episode had a self-contained storyline. The second series was a serial; the storyline developed over the episodes, which meant that if you were unlucky enough to miss one it was difficult to pick up what had happened. There was also no hut, so none of the claustrophobia and sense of captivity of the initial series. Having all the men sleeping in the same room at Thornley Manor never works as well.

The first episode, 'Return of the Seven: Part 1', did have its moments of brilliance. In fact, it contains one of the most memorable scenes in the show's history. Towards the end Oz, who previously has only been seen winding Barry up in the Falklands, and whose presence has been sorely missed, is shown on his return to England. The camera is fixed on Jimmy Nail's face, all of Oz's surliness and contempt pouring from his mangled mouth. It is not until the camera pulls back that we realize Oz is stark naked and about to suffer the indignity of a rectal examination. It's difficult to know who to pity more – Oz or the bloke donning the plastic gloves. It is a brilliant reintroduction to a brilliant character.

Oz: You know why I left this country in the first place don't you? I'll tell you. In a word, Margaret Bloody Thatcher, that's why, cos I'd had it, I was up to there with what she'd created. Bloody wasteland. Nae joy, nae hope, nae nowt. Young blokes get to 21 and they have never done a day's work in their lives; young kids can buy heroin in the bike sheds at school. But I thought 'Ah no, it cannot be as bad as what it was.' I was willing to give you lot the benefit of the doubt over this one, but what happens? What happens is that I've been back on my native soil for ten minutes, and I'm subjected to an act of fascist intimidation, cos that's what it is, you know, that's what it is, and I'll be writing to my MP about this.

Customs Officer: Spread!

Oz: What do you think you're going to find up there eh? A bloody new striker for Newcastle United?

All of a sudden it felt as if *Auf pet* was back. Until then the exposition of Dennis's, Neville's and Barry's domestic situations appeared to have slowed the show up. Once Oz was back the prospect of the reunion seemed more enticing. Not all the critics agreed; while most were filled with praise for its return, a few of the Thatcherite newspapers were unhappy at Oz's demagoguery. James Murray in the *Daily Express* led the sniffing.

'Do I detect a touch of electioneering in the savage outburst of Oz against Maggie Thatcher? She has turned the country, he roared, into "a bloody wasteland". Writer [sic] Ian La Frenais and Dick Clement should steer clear of contentious politics. They might alienate a lot of brickies.'

Auf pet groupies Nina Myskow in the *News of the World* and the *Daily Mirror*'s Hilary Kingsley had no such complaints. Myskow even managed to avoid a few obvious puns in singing the programme's praises.

'I must confess that I was worried about this second series: could it possibly match up to the brilliance of the first.

'It can and it does. And crikey, Central, hallelujah for that.

'It would be unfair to single any of them out: Oz, Barry, Moxie [sic] Nev, Bomber, Dennis and Wayne, they are REAL, to me.

'Such is the brilliance of the scripts, the perfection of the playing, that I find myself worrying about Dennis's drinking (he's got so boozy faced) and Neville's marriage.'

Kingsley was equally adulatory in her review, while Hugh Herbert in the *Guardian* was delighted to see the show return, even though, in an hilarious example of how bewildering Jimmy Nail's accent could be for those south of Watford, he believed that Oz asked the custom's officer about to search him whether he expected to find 'a new stand for Manchester United'.

'It's a welcome return on what can often be a bleak night on the box. Anything that makes you warm towards builders on any night of the week must contain some grain of magic.'

The show was a massive hit with the public: 15,392,000 people watched it, a whopping 30 per cent of the television audience. Of BARB's northeast viewing panel, 37 per cent tuned in. At 9 p.m., when Joe Fagin's latest anthem, 'Get It Right', kicked in, an extra 5 million people either turned to ITV or switched on their sets – a sign of how eagerly anticipated *Auf pet* was. *That's My Boy*, a sitcom featuring Mollie Sugden which was a lot more sit than com, had achieved barely 10 million viewers when it finished just before nine. The show trounced the opposition on BBC1: the news and the first series of *Lovejoy*. This was met with mixed feelings by Ian La Frenais, who had contributed several scripts for that first series, directed by Baz Taylor. In fact, a two-parter he wrote for *Lovejoy*, 'Death in Venice', was up against Episodes 3 and 4 of *Auf pet*.

It was inevitable, given its amazing start, that *Auf pet* would struggle to sustain such a high audience. Many viewers might have watched it for the first time and remained unimpressed. So Episode 2 garnered a 'mere' 13,703,000, while Episode 3 attained the lowest figures of the whole series with 13,342,000, still extremely pleasing for everyone involved.

The viewing figures soothed the worried brows of those who wondered how the new series would be received, given that the set-up and location were different. They need not have been concerned. What was clear was that the characters were so well loved by the public that they could have been filmed spotting trains and people would still have switched on to see them. The delights of the second series, and there are many, stem from the development of their personalities.

Given its rather pedestrian start, the series picks up once the lads are back together and are dispatched to transform Thornley Manor in the Midlands countryside. The series is helped not only by the wonderful acting by the existing members of the cast, but also by the addition of Bill Paterson's Ally Fraser. Fraser's presence, his fondness for wearing yellow jumpsuits aside, adds a crackle to the script and it is clear from the moment he appears that his involvement will only benefit the rest of the series. Paterson was, and is, one of the country's best television and film actors, as he'd shown in his role as Morris Wormold the meat inspector in *A Private Function*. As his girlfriend, the shallow, dizzy Vicky, Lesley St John, provided a perfect counterpoint.

Other actors make welcome guest appearances. Tim Healy's wife Denise Welch, who later went on to star in *Coronation Street*, plays the woman who is living in Oz's wife Marjorie's old flat

Above: One of the finest character actors of his generation, Bill Paterson, as Ally Fraser, with girlfriend Vicky, played by Lesley St John. Below: Wayne delivers his *coup de grâce* to his nemesis, Arthur – a video of his landlord's sexual escapades.

Bomber scales the walls of Thornley Manor.

James Booth receives some help with his backswing prior to filming a scene with Bill Paterson.

Tim Healy and Kevin Lloyd idle away time during a break in filming.

when Oz goes round to call. Geordie actress Gina Mckee has a minor two-line part as a victim of Wayne's charm in the country and western bar, one of her first roles in what is turning out to be a very successful career. Lovers of that great British film *Zulu*, will recognize James Booth, who played the malingering anti-hero Hook, in the role of the villainous Kenny Ames. Two actors who both died tragically young, Kevin Lloyd and Sammy Johnson, make appearances as brickies.

There are a few uneven moments during the brickies' clashes with Arthur Pringle, the landlord of the Barley Mow pub, played by the late Bryan Pringle. And some of the characters – like the snobbish, stuffy Arthur, a less psychotic and therefore less funny imitation of Basil Fawlty – were straight from central casting. The scene in which the gang brick up the front door of the pub and sing 'Wall Meet Again' down the phone to the enraged landlord became notorious when the press reported some real drinkers had inflicted a similar revenge on an officious landlord who had barred them from his premises.

Yet the Thornley Manor section contains some excellent touches and many of the series' best scenes, particularly when the lads clash *en masse* with the locals in a hotel bar. Barry gives away his hankering for social mobility by revealing to the class-conscious Neville that he is a member of the SDP ('It's the party of the future, that is mate') and refuses to acknowledge class barriers

Moxey, on the lam from the law, ponders life's complexities.

– until he agrees to relinquish his seat to the bristling Mr Trudaway who wishes to reclaim his stool. This in turn provokes a memorable rant from Oz at the preposterousness of such a claim.

'Are you trying to tell us that you bring that stool with you when you come oot? You get to the door with the stool under your arm and say, "I'm going over the pub for a pint, pet – with me stool." Eh?'

When they are told to leave Oz resists Barry's and Neville's suggestions that they slip away quietly. Instead, he returns to the bar for once last colourful rant at the pettiness and insularity of the middle classes.

'Where I come from, we welcome strangers. But yee lot, yee've made us welcome as a fart in an astronaut's suit.'

In another wonderful scene, while the rest of the seven depart to the pub Barry seeks to improve himself brass rubbing at a nearby church ('Got any suggestions, Blue Peter?'), a quintessential Barry moment. In another scene, again featuring Barry, Oz, bored at having to down tools, takes the nervous Brummie fishing, though without rods or nets. His method is to 'tickle' the fish. ('They're gutsy little bastards. They put up a fight.') In Episode 8, Oz asks Wayne to 'kidnap' his son Rod after a game of football while he diverts Sandro ('He must be a bit micey if he wants to lob up with our Marjorie'), the man who is whisking his wife away to Italy. Of course Wayne ends up with the wrong lad in the back of his BMW, which screeches to a halt shortly after setting off. Oz attempts to explain his *faux pas* to the bewildered schoolboy.

'Me and him are school board inspectors. And we go around testing kids like you, on their reflexes on things like this, and you've just failed. Miserably. However, we'll forget about this on the condition that you say nothing to your friends and we won't tell the headmaster. OK? Now, watch the road.'

While Oz and Barry get the best lines, the other characters continue to work around them. Wayne is ostracized for getting them kicked out of the pub because he has been sleeping with the landlord's daughter – a rather too predictable plot twist perhaps? Poor old Dennis does little except drink and look drunk, though Neville is as dependably wet as ever, feeling ever so slightly emasculated by Brenda's new job and her new-found desire to play badminton with junior doctors. Bomber is amiable enough, but has little to do. As Moxey, Chris Fairbank gets more to do and his character is fleshed out, constantly slipping away to London to gain another identity. Fairbank was pleased to be on the inside, not the periphery.

'I felt a part of it much more during that series, mainly because there was much more for my character to do. You got much more sense of his back story than in the first, and more of a sense of what he's about.'

Viewing figures for Episodes 4 and 5 remained around the 13,500,000 mark. This was too much for the BBC. In a pre-emptive attack they moved *Dynasty*, their flagship Friday night programme, to 8.30 p.m. from its usual slot at 8 p.m., which meant viewers would be forced to switch to ITV halfway through it to watch *Auf pet*, rather than being able to watch both shows as they had before. One can imagine the snide laughs in the BBC boardroom when they came up with that one.

It didn't work. In fact, it backfired spectacularly. *Dynasty* got 11,157,000 viewers, while *Auf pet* clung resolutely to its audience of around 13,500,000. Closer scrutiny of the figures shows just what a mistake the BBC had made. BARB splits each hour into quarters, so it is possible to see how the audience ebbs and flows during the course of a programme. At 8.45 p.m. 19 per cent of the viewing public were watching *Dynasty*, while 20 per cent were watching ITV. At 9 p.m. when *Auf pet* started, the share watching the BBC slumped to 14 per cent, while ITV's share soared to 26 per cent. A case of Auf Wiedersehen, Joan Collins!

The BBC didn't repeat its ruse the following week. *Dynasty* slunk back to its 8 p.m. slot, its shoulder pads between its legs. The result was that Episode 7, 'No Sex Please We're Brickies', got the highest figures of the series so far: 15,658,000. The next week, the show attained its highest audience ever when 16,017,000 people – 33 per cent of the viewing public – watched Oz return to Newcastle to prevent his son moving to Italy in 'Marjorie Doesn't Live Here Anymore', the most popular episode in *Auf pet*'s history. Coincidentally, replacing *Lovejoy* on BBC1 was a cold war mini-series called *Wynne and Penkovsky*, directed by Paul Seed who went on to direct the third series of *Auf pet*. By the next week, the episode before the action switches to Spain, the audience had

Oz demonstrates Geordie beachwear in all its glory.

settled at 15,108,000. In Spain the pace becomes more uneven. In Germany the comedy came from the lads being made to suffer, forced to get on their bikes to find a living and live cheek-by-jowl in a wretched hut. It is not easy to wring this kind of comedy out of scenes that saw them living the life any brickie would dream of – building a villa in the sun, knocking back the San Miguel. It is difficult to suggest they are in any way up against it. Their only real hardship is sharing their hotel with a party of highly-sexed octogenarians on a package holiday. And even Bomber seems to enjoy that.

The inconsistency of this section is partly explained by the death of Gary Holton, whose absence from many scenes is noticeable; he rarely appears in any interior ones. Again, there are magical moments like the group being found naked in the swimming pool of a pompous English couple, having mistaken it for Ally Fraser's villa. In Episode 10 they are dogged by unscrupulous journalists who believe them to be a gang of villains. In that sense it was a case of art imitating life, given that reporters hung around for most of the shoot in Spain. At the hotel bar, Barry tries to put a reptilian reporter off their scent with an ingenious cover story for their visit to Marbella.

Reporter: 'On holiday are we?'

Barry: (after hushing Oz) 'Sort of. We're a club, y'see.'

Reporter: 'What club is that then?'

Barry: 'It's the Wolverhampton and District Aqualung Society.'

Reporter: 'It's a long way from the sea, Wolverhampton.'

Barry: 'Oh yeah, how true. That's why this annual trip is so important to us, y'see. Oh yes, for the rest of the year we have to… make do… with the… reservoir… isn't that right lads?'

Oz: 'Aye, the reservoir.'

The show continued in similar form to its conclusion on 19 May. Despite the unevenness of the episodes, and the fact that it was clear many scenes had been rejigged to cover Holton's death, its popularity never once wavered and it attracted more viewers than the first series. Episode 10 drew an audience of 13,782,000 – slightly dented by coverage of world snooker at the Crucible on BBC2, as was Episode 11, which got 13,949,000. The upward trend continued for Episode 12, which was watched by just over 14 million people. Finally, 14,109,000 viewers tuned in to see Barry and Hazel get married aboard Ally Fraser's yacht with all the other lads acting as best men – Barry, true to form, not having been decisive enough to choose one. The cast and crew dedicated this last episode to Gary Holton, and before it was screened Tim Healy said a few words as a tribute. The decision was taken by the cast, who wanted to make a gesture.

In the press handkerchiefs were waved as TV reviewers said goodbye to the show. Maureen Paton in the *Daily Express* encapsulated many people's thoughts when she described it as 'one of the best comedy drama series ever made by British TV'. She also paid tribute to Jimmy Nail.

'I might even miss the spectacularly squalid Oz, though one could have done without him taking his clothes off at every opportunity.

'It is a tribute to Jimmy Nail's acting ability that he managed to make the great lumbering oaf rather endearing to masochists. And of course the rebel without a pause had all the best abrasive lines.

'Where this second series scored over the first was in the introduction of regular female characters and I am not being sexist.'

In the *Mirror* Hilary Kingsley called for another series. However, had she read Pauline Walch's piece in *Today* she might have seen that this was unlikely. The article mentioned that Jimmy Nail was keen to pursue a music career and that neither he nor Tim Spall had been approached to make a third series. A spokesman for Central was quoted as saying the matter would be discussed, but added the caveat: 'It could take a long time to get the artists and writers back together.' Fifteen years, in fact.

While the first series has stood the test of time, and still bears repeat viewing, the second has survived less well. Just as the actors and crew have different theories about why the first series was such a resounding a success, they have disparate opinions as to why the second series, though more popular, did not attain the same consistency.

Kevin Whately makes the pertinent point that, as a consequence of the problems that occurred during filming, it was inevitable that the show's quality would suffer.

'The scripts were just as brilliant as they always were, and in many ways on the page it was better than the first series. It's just that it didn't come across like that on screen because of things like Gary dying. It became a salvage exercise and a few of the episodes were cobbled together. It was a shame because those last three or four weeks of filming weren't much fun. No one went away thinking, "That was really fun, we should do it again," like they did after the first series.'

Dick Clement is unequivocal.

'I don't think it's anywhere near as good as the first. The story still holds up but it is a bit ambling in places. I think our writing is much tighter now. But the second series wasn't as pure as the first; it was more contrived. In many ways it was easier to write for the characters because the actors had put flesh on their bones, but it felt more awkward to write.'

La Frenais agrees with his writing partner.

'It is the weakest of the series. It didn't have the purpose of the first series. The characters were much more comfortable; the central premise took away the agenda of the first – like having to go away and live abroad, to be in a place they don't want to be. They all wanted to go to Spain and that was its weakness for me. Of course, it had its moments, and we had to keep a good storyline running through it, but it lacked the spine of the first series.'

Chris Fairbank subscribes to the theory that the series might not have been the best it could be, but that it was still a great show.

'Because of all the problems it was a case of just trying to get the damn thing made. All we wanted to do was get it in the can. The general feeling was that we had just about got away with it. We all felt it wasn't as good as the first one, but that it was still good because the characters were there. We discovered that it was the characters that the audience loved most of all, rather than the situation. In retrospect, I think people did like the fact they were in Germany and, perhaps more than that, they liked the fact we were all in a hut.'

Right: Barry and Hazel pose for their wedding photograph.

Gary Holton 1952–1985.

Roger Bamford still remains proud of the second series.

'The series was very difficult to shoot because of all the problems, and occasionally it was hell. But we got through it and I think what made the series was the ensemble. People loved those actors being together and those characters being together and the way they gel. The second series was more sprawling, but it worked.'

09: SPLITTING UP AND GOING ON SOLO

Once the critical acclaim had settled down and the series had ended, attention turned to whether there would be a third instalment. It swiftly emerged that there was little appetite among the cast for such an undertaking. As Kevin Whately pointed out, the last few weeks of filming had been such an arduous experience that there was little enthusiasm for another series. Without Gary Holton it would never be the same, anyway. Chris Fairbank says a few ideas were batted back and forth but came to naught.

'I thought I was in danger of being typecast, so I thought it might be good not to do any more and give myself the chance to work as an actor. Yet at the same time we had only done two series, so I think a third wouldn't have made much difference. I'm glad I wasn't faced with the decision of whether or not to do another. I've always subscribed to the maxim that you leave people wanting more. If you go on and on, you can cross an invisible line and once you've done that there is no going back.'

Kevin Whately says the prospect of being typecast wasn't the deciding factor for him either.

'We'd become seen as this amorphous bunch, 'the lads'. I think we all wanted to be seen as individuals. I wasn't bothered about being typecast because the more you're typecast then the more you work. Some actors like Tim Spall are great at playing a huge variety of parts, but most of us are selling one aspect of our character.'

People were keen to move on. *Auf pet* had given all the actors their breaks and they were finding themselves in demand, while other members of the team had projects they wished to pursue. Once it emerged that the cast would not be responsive to a third series, Clement and La Frenais moved on to other projects, though a couple of years later, while researching a *Lovejoy* script in Prague, the idea of reviving *Auf pet* occurred to both of them, as Dick Clement remembers.

'Little had been said about doing another series and we felt at the time two series was enough. It was either 1989 or 1990 and we saw a group of British brickies, including some Geordies, restoring the British Embassy in Prague. Ian and I looked at each other and said immediately, "It's our lads." Over dinner that evening we had the idea to write a one-off movie, perhaps set in Moscow behind the Iron Curtain, about the lads restoring the British Embassy. But it never came to more than that; a discussion between the two of us, a case of, "Wouldn't it be nice if…"'

According to Roger Bamford, after the troubles of the second series there was never any thought of doing another.

'I don't think we ever thought we'd do it again. There was definitely the feeling that we had got so far with it, that we had built it so high, that the only direction was down. I think this is where Tim Spall and Tim Healy, possibly Jimmy and Kevin, were looking at other things they wanted to do. We might have done it again had people insisted on it and paid lots of money, and it might have been a good show, but it might not have been as popular and it could have been a disaster. I would have hated to do it actually.

'I don't think we ever said, "Right, that's it. It's over." We all knew we'd meet again. I don't think we expected to do it again, though. That group that started in that chilly little hut were a very different group by the end. They were all off doing their own thing. But we reached the top and there is nowhere you can go from there, apart from down the other side, so I was happy that it ended there.'

However, the *Auf pet* story doesn't quite come crashing to a halt here. In 1986, Healy and Nail took part in a Tyne Tees Television production about the dangers of AIDS. Entitled *Educating Oz*, the purpose of the 25-minute film was to raise awareness of the disease – which was minimal and not helped by the prevailing attitude that it only affected gays. This myth was propagated by Kelvin McKenzie's *Sun*, which once ran a leader that said: 'Forget the idea that ordinary heterosexual people can contract AIDS. They can't … anything else is just homosexual propaganda.' (The newspaper was later censured and forced to concede that it was wrong.) Dealing with views and prejudices similar to those presented by the *Sun* was the aim of the short film.

The premise is that Dennis has been asked to give a talk to 70 bricklayers about the dangers of AIDS. He has attended a course and afterwards goes to a pub to watch the course leader being interviewed on television. Of course, Oz is in the pub and has little time for Dennis's worries about the disease. ('I mean I can't understand how a woman can give it to a man, cos it's, well, it's one way traffic when you get in there isn't it?') After failing to overcome his friend's bigotry, Dennis calls in the help of a doctor and in the end, lo and behold, Oz is made to see the merits of contraception.

Once the actors had moved on to different projects the chances of reuniting them became less likely. Jimmy Nail pursued his music career with vigour and a certain amount of success – he had a huge number one hit with 'Ain't No Doubt'. He also appeared in several films, and wrote and starred in two popular TV shows: *Spender*, a tale of a gloomy Geordie investigator which ran for three seasons; and *Crocodile Shoes*, about a lathe operator who dreams of making it as a country and western singer. *Spender* was created with the help of La Frenais and became a staging post for *Auf pet* alumni. Among the cast and crew were the likes of Chris Fairbank, Tim Spall, Sammy Johnson, Denise Welch and Berwick Kaler (who played Vera's new boyfriend, Alan, in the first series of *Auf pet*). Behind the camera, Roger Bamford and Martin McKeand were also involved; and Stan Hey penned a couple of episodes. Chris Fairbank also appeared in both series of *Crocodile Shoes*. On the big screen, Spall and Nail appeared together in 1988 as a pair of unscary demons in a dodgy horror film called *Dream Demons*.

Spall, undoubtedly the best actor of the group, went on to fulfil his potential. On TV he appeared as the titular hero of *Frank Stubbs Promotes* and, in one of the best television performances of recent times, he played an impassioned picture archivist in Stephen Poliakoff's *Shooting the Past*. In the movies he has acted in several Mike Leigh films, most notably *Secrets and Lies*, and at the time of writing this book he was in Australia completing the filming of *The Last Samurai* with Tom Cruise.

A year after *Aufpet* ended Kevin Whately landed the role of Lewis in *Inspector Morse* alongside John Thaw. The show ran for more than a decade and cemented the Geordie as one of Britain's best-loved actors. He turned up in the Oscar-winning *The English Patient* and featured in several TV shows, though he is the only member of the Aufpet team not to have acted in one with any of the others. 'Jimmy wanted me to play a villain in *Spender*,' he recalls, 'but it never got round to happening.'

Chris Fairbank went back to being, in his own words, 'what I always was: a jobbing actor'. Some of his jobs weren't too bad, though. He won bit parts in blockbusters such as *Batman*, *The Fifth Element* and *Alien 3* as well as doing a vast amount of television. He also travelled to Zimbabwe to film *White Hunter, Black Heart*, directed by Clint Eastwood. Tim Spall was involved too, 'though we never met on that,' he remembers.

Tim Healy proved himself to be one of the country's best comic actors in shows such as *Boys from the Bush* and *Common as Muck*, and appeared in the film *Purely Belter*. He also makes a memorable cameo appearance in the first episode of Peter Kay's excellent *Phoenix Nights*. As the lead singer of a folk group, Healy sings a racist song that ruins the opening night of Brian Potter's new club.

Pat Roach, by his own admission not a full-time actor, was seen less often on television. But he scored a hat-trick of Indiana Jones appearances when he turned up as a gestapo agent in *The Last Crusade*, the final part of the trilogy. That wasn't the end of his blockbuster roles: he played a Celtic chieftain in *Robin Hood: Prince of Thieves*. Off the screen he cemented his reputation as a bit of an entrepreneur, running a health club and other businesses. At the time of writing this book he was trying to persuade his fellow cast members to record an album of their favourite Christmas carols, an idea that brought much eye rolling and shaking of heads from the prospective singers. Chris Fairbank marvels at some of the ideas Roach has had, one in particular.

'Pat always has these ideas; he's full of them. One of the best was when he came in one day and said [adopting a Brummie accent], "Listen fellas. You know the Brits and how they love their pets? Well, I've got an idea. We should club together and open a cemetery for pets. We could call it, Auf Wiedersehen, Pets." There was a silence. I said, "How are we going to promote this venture, Pat? Stand there holding a dead dog and a dead cat in each hand?"'

The last regular member of the team, Julia Tobin, gave up acting altogether a few years after the second series of Aufpet was screened. She gave birth to a son and was understandably reluctant to go away on location as a result, so she confined herself to the odd voice-over and a life of domestic bliss. As a friend of Madelaine Newton she kept in touch with other members of

Cast members gather in London for the press screening of series two.

the cast, Whately in particular, and because everyone else was doing so well, it never crossed her mind that Brenda would ever return.

All the cast were busy and no-one had to worry too much about money. Many of them continued to act together and kept in touch, so the bond between the lads was maintained. Occasionally, the whole *Auf Pet* team was reunited. The first time was when the show won the 'Best Drama of the Decade' award from *TV Times*. The second was when they met up in 1995 to celebrate all 26 episodes being repeated on Channel 4. The series had previously been rerun by ITV on several occasions – most memorably when it was edited down into half-hour episodes and Oz's language was censored because it was shown opposite the BBC's *EastEnders*. It made little impact and quite right too; an expurgated Oz is of little use to anyone. As Chris Fairbank remembers, 'With all the ball scratching and language cut out, Oz hardly makes an appearance.'

Had you put the prospect of another series to any of the six actors the response would have been a vigorous shake of the head – the will simply wasn't there. To find the money to pay their wages and please their agents would take an effort of Herculean proportions; and finding a time when all their diaries would coincide and free them to spend four or five months filming seemed impossible from a logistical point of view. For these reasons, Kevin Whately truly believed that *Auf pet* was dead.

'There was no way I saw us getting back together. Never. It was mostly just a time thing. We were all so busy all the time that it seemed impossible to get us back together. I'm not sure it ever crossed my mind that we'd get back together again. I remember being glad they kept repeating it though, for the money [laughs].'

Fairbanks says people often asked him if there would be another series and he was always adamant in his reply.

'Over the years people would occasionally say, "Shame you didn't do anything else. Any chance you might get back together?" I suppose it was a reflection of the esteem in which the show was held. Furthermore, it was testament to the quality of the writing. It has turned out to be like a fine wine in that it has improved with age. When Channel 4 ran both series the remarkable thing was how well it stood up. There was the thought it might be creaking, showing its age. But I was amazed that, apart from a few obvious Eighties references, it stood up stronger then anything else on television at the time.

'I never thought it would happen again though. Never. Jimmy was doing music and had got well stuck into *Spender* and all of that stuff. Spally was off making movies, Kev was doing loads of stuff and Tim Healy was being really successful. I'd put the show behind me and got down to working on whatever came up.'

Tim Healy felt the same.

'We never dreamed of doing any more because we never needed to. I've had a good career since then. It was the best thing that ever happened to me; it was like a trampoline. I must have done seven TV series since then, not that people remember them like they remember *Auf Wiedersehen, Pet*, but I've just worked and worked and worked. That holds true for most if us; we just wanted to go off and forge our own careers, which we managed to do.'

Perhaps it is because all the actors had proved themselves in their own right that they did not entirely dismiss the idea of returning to the characters who had made them famous when it was put to them. That the show was resurrected did come as a surprise. But then it was a strange combination of death, desire and perseverance that enabled this legendary television programme to return.

10: BACK WITH THE BOYS AGAIN

Two events, entirely unrelated, started the process that saw *Auf pet* being brought back to life. First, towards the end of 1999 Franc Roddam was informed that the rights for the programme had reverted to him. Following a spell living and working in Hollywood he was back in London, working as a producer on a few film ideas. The movie business is notoriously cumbersome in the way it operates; sometimes it can take two or three years to raise the money to fund a production. Understandably, Roddam was eager to get a more immediate project off the ground; something that wouldn't be held up by red tape and disagreements about money and directors. He began to think about reviving *Auf pet*, though he knew it would have to be different from the first two series. Simply rehashing his original idea wouldn't work.

In a way, he'd been on the outside while the show became a success. He is very proud of the way it was received by the public and, in particular, how it launched the successful careers of such a talented group of actors. His successful career in the movies offset any regrets he had at not bringing the programme to the screen himself.

'My input wasn't big in the first series and it was non-existent during the second. I was busy making films, plus, being a director myself, I didn't want to get in the way of another director. I'm the sharp end of the spear in a way. I sometimes think that if I hadn't followed through with the idea, had I not taken it to Allan McKeown and then Dick and Ian, there would have been no Jimmy Nail, there would be no Kevin Whately. On the other hand I have to acknowledge the fantastic contribution by Dick and Ian – they brought it to life so brilliantly – and the actors, the directors, the casting directors that made it a success.

'I wasn't too surprised when it became the success it was. What was never in doubt was the quality of the writing and the quality of the cast. I never doubted the idea and if I have a good idea I try to make it happen. That's what I do now. I try to move energy around. I take my initial energy for a project and try to enthuse others; I could quite easily have dropped *Auf pet* at any time, but I wanted to keep it going, so I passed that enthusiasm on to Dick and Ian and they then passed that on to Roger Bamford and the cast.'

Roddam went back to the beginning for inspiration. What had awakened his interest in the original concept was that to him it symbolized the end of the industrial age, the switch from blue-collar to white-collar work – a transition that left behind a whole generation of men. He started playing around with the idea that a new series might deal with another transition – this time the birth of the electronic age, and how that was leaving behind yet another generation of men. But the concept wasn't yet 'coming through'. However, he did have a working relationship with Alan Yentob, Director of Drama and Entertainment at the BBC. Over lunch one day he happened to mention the idea of bringing back *Auf pet*. Would the BBC be interested? Yentob said that if Roddam was able to reunite the whole cast, and Clement and La Frenais, he might be interested.

Recruiting Whately, Nail, Healy, Fairbank, Roach and Spall would not be the easiest task in the world. But what Roddam wasn't aware of was an event that had made three of the actors realize just how much affection the public still had for the show.

Sammy Johnson was a widely respected actor and an integral part of the Geordie Mafia. He was also Tim Healy's best friend – the pair met while working with Live Theatre. In *Auf pet* he'd played Martin Cooper, the hated brickie selected to replace the missing Moxey for the trip to Spain until the Scouser's much welcomed return. In *Spender* he played the hero's sidekick, 'Stick', and he'd also starred in *Crocodile Shoes* with Nail. In 1999, while in Malaga training for the Great North Run, he died of a heart attack. He was 48.

Tim Healy was devastated. Johnson was 'like a brother' to him. He remembers how, shortly after his friend's death, Nail came to see him.

'He said to me, "Why don't you do something for him?" I said, "What do you mean?" He said, "Why don't you put a park bench for him, stick it in Jesmond Dean. Or why don't you set up a fund for him?" I thought that was a good idea, so I rang up the community foundation who set up trust funds. I asked Jim if he'd come and do a show with me at the city hall in Newcastle. He said he would. The Sammy Johnson Memorial Fund was set up and on February sixth in 2000 we held a concert for it.'

Sammy Johnson pictured with Jimmy Nail in *Spender*.

Nail agreed to approach Clement and La Frenais to ask if they would contribute a few sketches for him, Healy and Whately, who had also been approached, to do as Oz, Dennis and Neville. The writers agreed, wrote three sketches and sent them to Nail. Healy and Whately went around to Nail's London home to rehearse. According to Whately, 'It was great fun just reading Dick and Ian's scripts again; they were really funny.'

The concert started with an introduction by Tim Healy. This was followed by a few songs from Johnson's old band, the evocatively named Pig Meat. Then there was a gigantic roar from the 2,500 people in the audience as the lights went down and Joe Fagin's gravel voice singing 'Breaking Away' filled the auditorium. Mike Neville, the voice of *North East News*, was the narrator. 'The year is 1983,' he said. 'The place: Düsseldorf.'

The lights went up to reveal Whately and Healy onstage. The crowd responded as if Newcastle had just won the Premiership by beating Sunderland, at home, 8–0, thereby condemning them to relegation and probable bankruptcy. Here, thanks to Dick Clement and Ian La Frenais, are the sketches written for that reunion.

Act One — Frankfurt airport
Neville is revealed at a payphone, dressed against the
cold in anorak and jeans.

NEVILLE Just tell her it's Neville, she'll accept the
charges... Brenda?... At Frankfurt airport, pet. I'm
coming home. Well, we all are, the job's over. Should
be back about tea time, I'll fill you in then, pet, it's
our phone bill... Love you too.

He puts down the phone as Dennis appears, a duty-free bag
in one hand and a cup of coffee in the other.

NEVILLE (CONT'D) Brenda says hello.
DENNIS Oh aye? She'll be surprised we're going home ahead
of schedule.
NEVILLE Aye.
DENNIS D'you tell her the hut burned down and we lost all
our gear?
NEVILLE I thought I'd hold back on that one.
DENNIS What, till after you've shown her your tattoo?
NEVILLE Don't remind me...
DENNIS Howway, she'll probably find it sexy, man. I
mean, Sean Connery's got one.
NEVILLE Sean Connery hasn't got one sayin' 'Neville and
Lotte' on his bicep.
DENNIS Listen, she knows why you did this job, and the
graft involved.
NEVILLE S'pose so. I mean, I've been sending good money
home.
DENNIS It was a good gig. And the Germans weren't so bad.

Backstage at this point was an extremely nervous Jimmy Nail. Whately says all three were
'shitting themselves', but Nail had never acted live onstage. Offstage his voice was heard to shout,

'They were still Germans though, but!' The place roared with delight, a noise that got louder when Nail, as Oz, walked onstage wearing a scruffy T-shirt and carrying a duty-free bag. Whately compares the sound to that of a plane taking off. The sketch continues.

```
DENNIS Aw, come on, Oz.
OZ They're still the bastards who bombed my granny.
DENNIS They gave us work when there was none at home.
You've probably forgotten, in an alcoholic haze, but
that's what this trip was about! And most of us are better
off now than when we left.

Neville nods in agreement.

NEVILLE You'd be surprised how much I've managed to put
away.
OZ Bet it's less coin than Gazza gets in a week.
NEVILLE It's a lot to me.
OZ Enough to make a down payment on that poncy little
bungalow in Ponteland?
NEVILLE What's wrong with that?
OZ Have you ever been to Ponteland?
NEVILLE Course I have.
OZ It's scary, really scary. Hush Puppies and Hermes
scarves. Like the Midwich cuckoos all grew up.
DENNIS It's better than the council house he lives in
now! That's the point of it all, Oz. Our dads left us
more than they had, an' we'll leave our kids more than
we've got.
OZ And you think you're gonna get that through honest
graft?
```

There was a pause here. The audience started to giggle in anticipation of what was coming next.

```
OZ That's a load of bollocks, Dennis.
```

At this point the crowd erupted with delight. Whately and Healy almost corpsed but managed to rein themselves in. Healy stepped out of character for a second to say to Nail, 'You've waited for that, haven't you?' Once the laughter died down the sketch continued.

OZ The working man doesn't have any nobility. Not under Thatcher. You get money through guile, cunning, luck or bein' a drug dealer.
DENNIS Oh, we'll put our wedge into that then. Flog it round the estates. 'Special offers on heroin this week!'

Oz shakes his head — these two aren't getting it.

OZ Lemme tell you a story me dad told us. 'Bout this Greek bloke who jumped ship and settled in North Shields. His name was Tommy Carlisle and he lived in a seamen's hostel —
DENNIS Hang on. You said he was Greek. And he's called Tommy Carlisle?
OZ He changed his name, didn't he? Made it easier than bein' Dimitri Something-opoulos.
NEVILLE But why Carlisle?
OZ I've no idea, Neville.
NEVILLE He obviously hadn't been there.
OZ Well he probably hadn't.
NEVILLE I once spent a whole Sunday there.
OZ D'you want to hear this story or don't you?
NEVILLE Not bothered.
DENNIS Aw, get on with it, man.
OZ The point is: he lived out of dustbins. And he'd find things that people hoyed away. Like a three-legged chair or a broken toy. So he'd mend 'em, and sell 'em. Put away a penny or two. Then he made himself a little handcart. Collected more stuff. In a year he had a horse-drawn cart. Was working from Walker to Smiths Dock. And you know how much he's worth today?

Neville and Dennis exchange looks, guessing millions.

DENNIS Go on then, tell us.
OZ Nothing!

BLACKOUT.

Another act took to the stage before there was another blackout and hubbub filled the auditorium.

Act Two — Malaga airport
In the darkness we hear a chime, followed by an announcement, first in Spanish, then accented English:

VOICE Iberian Airlines regrets to announce that Flight 391 to London Gatwick is delayed due to the late arrival of the aircraft.

A date is projected: '1987'.
And once again, Neville is revealed at a payphone. His anorak has been replaced by a summer shirt and a tan, if time allows. (If not, at least the lighting should be warmer.)

NEVILLE Just tell her it's Neville, por favor... (pause) Brenda? It's me... We're still at Malaga, pet. Flight's been delayed. I bought some castanets for your mother at the gift shop... (then, hurt) Well, I dunno, she can find some use for them, surely? I'll call you from Gatwick — if we ever get there.

He puts the phone down as Oz appears in shorts and a golf hat, with more duty-free and a copy of the Sun.

OZ Says here there's rumours we might sell Gascoigne.
NEVILLE They wouldn't dare. Be riots in the streets.
OZ I don't understand them. But then I don't understand a lot of things in life. Duran Duran, to name but two.
NEVILLE Least we'll see a match Saturday.
OZ Oh that's a great consolation. Don't you realize something, Neville? We're in worse shape now than we were three years ago when we left Germany. The only thing we got out of Spain was sunburn. We lost a whole month's wages and our bonus. Still believe in honest graft?
NEVILLE Yes I do! It was because we tried to cut corners, this happened. We knew the boss was a crook going in. But we thought we'd save the tax and get away with it - well, we didn't.

Oz shakes his head.

OZ Still chasing that dream house?
NEVILLE We've found a place in Killingworth.
OZ Bit of a comedown from Ponteland.
NEVILLE Bollocks!

Dennis appears, looking serious. He's feeling responsible for the situation.

DENNIS So listen, I just spoke to this agent in London. There's a big job if we want in. Desalination plant in Saudi.
NEVILLE What's that mean?
DENNIS I've no idea, but it's top whack.
NEVILLE Saudi! It's so... far.
OZ And hot. And sandy. And they lop your dick off if you look at their women.

NEVILLE I dunno, Dennis. I'd sooner find something back home.

DENNIS You never will. They've pissed on people like you and me back home. Back home is for people in suits who work in the City and make money for the sake of making more money. People who ride their Range Rovers to their country houses on Friday nights, and get Concorde to Barbados when the weather gets a bit chilly. It's for those bastards, not us.

Oz and Neville exchange looks, surprised by this outburst.

OZ Sounding a bit bitter, Dennis.

DENNIS I just feel bad about what's happened. It was me put this team together. Anyway, what do you think? Bomber and Moxey want in.

NEVILLE How much would it be?

DENNIS Two K a month, basic. Before overtime.

NEVILLE I'd need to go home first. Discuss it with Brenda and get some clean shirts.

DENNIS What about you, Oz? One last job? Put us in the clear?

OZ Don't think so. Know what I think I'll do? I met this lass in a bar the other night. She's from Barcelona. Said if I was ever round her way. So I might just tool up there.

DENNIS What? You'd give up a job like this for a shag in Barcelona?

OZ I'd give up Saudi Arabia for a shag in Wallsend, Dennis.

NEVILLE And what about when your money runs out?

OZ I'll worry about that then. I'm 30, and I'm not spending a year of me life in the desert with a lot of towelheads telling me I can't have a drink. I'm gonna see about changing me flight.

He exits. Dennis shakes his head.

DENNIS Hopeless case. He'll never change.
NEVILLE This would be the last one, Dennis, right? I mean, Brenda and me want to start a family.
DENNIS This way you'll have something to give 'em, won't you?
NEVILLE Aye.
DENNIS C'mon, I'll buy you a beer.

They pick up their things and start to walk off. As the lights dim we hear Neville:

NEVILLE Did you hear they want to sell Gazza?!

BLACKOUT.

Then it was time for the night's final sketch, bringing the *Auppet* story up to date.

Act Three - Newcastle aiport
In the darkness we hear a chime, followed by a slightly refined, female Geordie voice:

VOICE This is the first call for British Airways Flight BA 435 for London Heathrow, boarding at Gate Three.

Once again a date is projected: '1999'.

Lights discover Neville and Dennis. They're both wearing shell suits and talking into cellular phones.

NEVILLE ... So you and your sister look after the baby for me now. And don't give your mam any trouble, OK...
DENNIS ... No, no, two tickets, in the name of Patterson and Hope... Yes, right. I'll pick them up when I get to Heathrow at the Aeroflot desk...
NEVILLE ... Love you too.

He blows a kiss into the phone and both men snap their phones shut simultaneously.

DENNIS Kids all right?
NEVILLE Could hardly hear them for Puff Daddy.

Dennis vibes Neville's familiar frown.

DENNIS You all right?
NEVILLE Not really.
DENNIS Cold feet?
NEVILLE I'm sure they will be where we're going.
DENNIS It's only six months, man.
NEVILLE And they're putting us up in a hotel?
DENNIS Three star, he said.
NEVILLE Good. 'Cos I don't want to go through what we went through in Gdansk.
DENNIS No way, son.

Some passengers come through from an arriving flight. These could include celebrities who are in the show, such as Alan Shearer... And then a familiar figure - except he's not all that familiar, the lads don't even recognize him. It's Oz! A new, improved, streamlined Oz. New wardrobe, new hair - maybe a bit too much gold about the wrists. He recognizes the lads and comes over.

OZ Dennis! Neville!

DENNIS Bloody hell — Oz!

NEVILLE I haven't seen you in yonks.

OZ Haven't been up here for years.

DENNIS Well, where're you livin' then?

OZ Aw, y'know, I've been moving around a lot. Miami, the last three months. So how's Brenda?

NEVILLE Great.

OZ Bairns?

NEVILLE Three. All girls. Hailey, Philippa, and the new baby, Calista.

OZ Wow. What about you, Dennis? Marry again?

DENNIS Naw. Well I was for a while. So what you doing up here?

OZ Me sister's not been very well, so I bought her a new house. In Ponteland.

Neville can't believe this — and doesn't want to. Oz registers their hand luggage.

OZ (CONT'D) So where are you two off to?

NEVILLE (hesitantly) Azer-bai... er...

DENNIS Azerbaijan.

OZ Where's that?

NEVILLE I'm still not sure. Can't find it on my atlas...

DENNIS It's east of Turkey. We fly to Moscow, then Moscow to Baku.

OZ Oh, I've heard of Baku. They played Sunderland once, so I was rooting for them. What are you going there for?

DENNIS (quickly) Holiday...

NEVILLE (picking up his cue) Yeah, y'know, Brenda's got the new baby, Dennis was free and we thought, somewhere not too touristy.

DENNIS It's right on the Caspian Sea. Great for snorkelling, that kind of thing...

Oz sees something sticking out of the top of Neville's grip.

OZ So what's the spirit level for?

Both of them are angry at being caught out in their lie.

DENNIS Alright, we're going there for work, okay?!
NEVILLE Power station.
DENNIS But there's still a lot of great snorkelling apparently!
OZ Fine, good. Did a lot of that in Florida. Down the Keys, y'know.
NEVILLE No, I don't know.
OZ Bit of marlin fishing too... (he mimes reeling in a big catch) Fantastic.

Dennis can't take this any more.

DENNIS Look, they've called our flight, so we haven't got long, but I have to know. Have you cracked it, Oz?
OZ I have, Den, yes.
NEVILLE (anguished) How?
OZ Well, after Spain I didn't have a pot to piss in. But then me mam died.
NEVILLE Life insurance?
OZ Don't be daft! For years a man in a raincoat came once a week and she gave him a shilling.
DENNIS (exasperated) What then?
OZ Well, she had this little shed in her garden. And the

bloke next door said 'I'll give you ten quid for that.'
Made me think of you, Dennis. And what you always said
about grafting for a living.
DENNIS I don't follow.
OZ I took the ten quid and I built two sheds. 'Cos all
the people round there, they haven't any room for their
spare stuff. An' I sold those for twenty quid. Made four
sheds. Now I've got forty quid. Pretty soon I've taken
on a lad and we're turning out twenty sheds a week.
NEVILLE And that's how you did it?
OZ No, then I won the Lottery and I said 'Fuck the sheds'.

BLACKOUT.

The evening ended with the veteran Geordie band Lindisfarne performing a rendition of their anthem 'Fog On the Tyne' – thankfully without Paul Gascoigne's awful rapping – augmented by backing vocals from Nail, Whately and Healy and the rest of the company. The night had been a joyous one and money had been raised in Johnson's name. Whately recalls that none of the three could believe their reception.

'It was like being in the middle of a volcano. It made my hair stand up on the back of my neck. It was such a thrill. Jimmy said afterwards, "I'd forgotten how much fun this was." Then he mentioned the idea of doing an *Auf Wiedersehen* film, a one-off and both Tim and I said we were up for it. But it was the adrenalin talking. I'm not sure any of us was that serious.'

Healy remembers the commitment being more definite than that.

'The whole place went ape shit as soon as we all appeared onstage and Jimmy got some great laughs. When we all came off we agreed it was brilliant. Within a week he was on the phone to me saying, "Fancy doing another?" Hearing that from Jimmy was unbelievable. It was the love and warmth from that crowd that made the three of us think more positively about doing it again. Without that response, I'm not sure what that happened next would have gone ahead.'

What happened next was that Roddam and Nail bumped into each other by accident. Roddam and Nail are represented by the same agency and Roddam had already made tentative inquiries about whether Nail would be interested in doing another series. 'You'll never get him,' the producer was told unequivocally. But he knew that if he managed to persuade Nail of the merits of the idea, recruiting the others might not be so difficult. He was not aware of the benefit concert and he was certainly unaware that Nail had been talking enthusiastically of persuading Dick and Ian to write a film updating the *Auf pet* story.

As Roddam left a bathroom shop on All Saints Road in Notting Hill – the road that gave its name to the girl band All Saints – he saw Nail coming out of a guitar shop across the street. It had been a while since the two had spoken and they greeted each other warmly. Roddam then broached the subject of *Auf pet*. 'I've got the rights,' he told Nail. 'I'm thinking of bringing it back.' 'Well, I'm up for it,' Nail said. Over a cup of coffee Roddam told him of Alan Yentob's interest, but added they would have to guarantee that all six of the surviving members of the cast would be willing to return. Otherwise there would be no chance of reviving the show. 'Let me call the guys,' Nail said. Roddam agreed, knowing that Nail stood a better chance of persuading any waverers than he did. The pair then discussed what to do about a storyline. They knew Clement and La Frenais were busy writing and rewriting movies, and that it would be difficult to persuade them to find time to write a series from scratch even if they were interested in another one. 'What if we came up with an idea and sold it to them,' Roddam said. Nail agreed. Having written both *Spender* and *Crocodile Shoes*, he knew what was required. The pair agreed to meet up again once Nail had rung round the rest of the group.

For Chris Fairbank, the call came completely out of the blue.

'Jimmy told me about Franc Roddam, the possible involvement of the BBC. Then he said, "I don't want to say too much now but I just wanted to see whether you were up for it." I asked him what the others had said and he said they'd been positive. So I said, "If all the others are saying yes then it would be rude not to." I felt quite excited about it. Then as soon as I put the phone down a few doubts crept in. I suddenly felt all the reasons for not doing it; how the cynics would use phrases like, "wasting the licence-payer's money", "out-of-work actors with nothing else to do other than rehash old ideas". I was quite uncertain.'

Pat Roach agreed without hesitation; Healy, memories of Newcastle city hall still vivid in his mind, also indicated his enthusiasm, as did Timothy Spall. Kevin Whately, like Fairbank, had misgivings.

'It crossed my mind that the critics would be sharpening their knives. None of us had wanted to do another series, though we thought a one-off might be fun. I wasn't sure if a series would work, but I sort of said I was interested.'

The idea for the series was developing. Roddam knew it had to be on a grand scale, so he started thinking big. In the gym one morning he came across a property developer from Teeside. They fell into conversation about the newly built Riverside Stadium in Middlesbrough. The property developer spoke about a piece of land on the other side of the river that was ripe for development. The only problem was the Transporter Bridge was in the way. 'If that bridge was moved, there'd be all that land to develop,' he said.

Roddam was inspired. The Transporter was a local landmark, part of his upbringing. To move it was unthinkable. But it would make a great plot. Move it where though? Roddam had made a film, *War Party*, during which he spent nine months living on a native American reservation. He'd become fascinated with the casinos, the sole source of income for the people who lived there. Over time the idea came together. Roddam pictured the meeting of two great lost tribes: native Americans and British working-class men. He and Nail met to write and develop the concept. Nail had the idea that Barry had become a millionaire from selling out-of-date food, and also that Oz's son was gay. Inspired, they sat facing each other across a table in Roddam's house in Notting Hill, and wrote a 'bible', a 160-page book that would provide the basis for any scripts that would be written. Roddam says it was great writing with Nail.

'He has a great ear for dialogue and he's very meticulous. He'll question a script. Dick and Ian have been living in LA for years but Jimmy is still connected with the street, how people talk. He's a great writer in his own right, but getting him involved in writing the 'bible' brought him in and meant he was involved with the project from the start, which was great, because he's a really strong character.'

Then it was time to ring Clement and La Frenais. Roddam says their reaction was initially negative – understandably. They had established themselves as writers for the movies and were phenomenally busy. There was no need for them to jeopardize their reputations reviving a show that was almost two decades old. La Frenais says the risk didn't seem worth it.

'When it was first suggested I thought, "That's a terrible idea. The British press are so awful they will accuse us of recycling old ideas." It seemed a perilous venture and after that phone call I didn't see it happening.'

Nail and Roddam were not to be denied. They undertook a ten-day road trip through Arizona as research, so that Nail could meet the native Americans, see the scenery and experience the casinos. Halfway through, Clement and La Frenais agreed to join up with them. Roddam was slowly gaining their interest.

'It's positive manipulation. I thought, "If I can get them to Arizona for a few days and the more we get together, the more momentum we get." I kept trying to push it on. I mean, just being in Arizona is inspiring. It's so beautiful. I wanted that contrast between the grey drabness of Middlesbrough and the luminous reds of the canyons and the blue skies in Arizona. I remember taking a photograph of the Transporter Bridge and showing it to some BBC executives. They looked at it and said, "Oh what a beautiful black-and-white photograph." I said, "It's in colour. That's 'Boro!"'

Roddam and Nail pitched their idea to Clement and La Frenais. The writing pair were impressed. Much like the meeting in the Café Moustache almost 20 years before, they sparked ideas of their own, set them thinking about ways to develop the story. La Frenais was impressed by the sheer scale of the project.

'The idea of moving the Transporter Bridge was such a monstrously large one that it appealed. There had to be something a bit over the top to hook the series on, rather than just having the lads work on a building site again. The idea was high-risk, it was entrepreneurial, it was big, and that advanced the guys from where we'd seen them last. The idea was so ludicrous that we thought, "We'd better do this." Dick and I started thinking about it, and what was most appealing was doing what we call "the round up". Inventing what they had been doing for all these years and how to get them back together again.'

Dick Clement was astounded at how much work Nail and Roddam had put into the idea.

'They had spent so much time on it, and it acted as a great starter motor for Ian and me. Some of the stuff was great; the bridge idea, Barry being rich, the gay son. It was all great stuff and it really got our juices going. I loved Franc's idea about the American Indians; it was inspired, and I give Franc all the credit for that. It made for that culture clash we were always seeking, and he made the analogy between the two displaced tribes. It was truly imaginative.'

There had been a sticking point with Timothy Spall. Not because he did not want to be involved, just that he was so busy it seemed impossible to find a time when he could be. According to Roddam, his agent was keen to protect her client's movie career and prevent him becoming saddled with a character he'd long left behind. Nevertheless, knowing he had the tacit agreement of both cast and writers, Roddam was able to return to Alan Yentob and ask him to finance another series. Without hesitation, Yentob did, though no scripts were written. Roddam was then able to return to the actors and their agents and say a deal was on the table. It took six months of negotiations but eventually all six were contracted for a third series of *Auf pet*.

To gird everyone's loins, Roddam organized the meal at the Mirabelle during which La Frenais outlined the idea. They all came away reassured about what they were about to embark on, sharing the aim that it would be bigger and better than the previous two series, and impressed by the BBC's commitment. After all, Yentob had picked up the bill.

One of the main problems that arose from the meal was the 'Wayne' question. All the actors were adamant that no one should be cast in Holton's place. Therefore his absence had to be adequately explained. Back in LA the writers gave the problem much thought. Their eventual solution was that Wayne had died and would be replaced by his son, Wyman, whose reason for joining the group would be that they all knew his dad, while he never had. Clement explains their decision.

'We could have said, "Wayne's emigrated. He's gone to Australia." But we decided to deal with it directly and give it a slight poignancy. All of us wanted to be respectful to Gary's memory.'

La Frenais says Nail was at first resistant to the idea of the son. Would it work? Eventually, he agreed that it would. With that problem solved the writers set about writing the scripts. They were delighted to still hear the characters' voices in their heads. La Frenais remembers that some were easier to recapture than others.

'The biggest problem was Oz. We knew the audience liked Oz for being Oz, but everyone changes in 15 years. The problem was how to make him different. He was behind the whole scheme, so obviously he'd developed some entrepreneurial nous, but we also had to try and preserve some of the old Oz, especially in certain situations. It was difficult to find the voice. We kept seeing Jimmy Nail and all the differences between him now and what he was like 15 years ago. He used to be this big working-class lad and since then he's been on the cover of *GQ* magazine. It was hard to balance what Oz had become with how much of the old Oz existed.'

Bringing the story up to date was another problem. La Frenais agrees that although he and Clement visit England three or four times a year, it is occasionally difficult to keep up with societal changes, to find out what has gone on – which is where Nail and Roddam helped. The writers also increased the frequency of their visits. Clement says they wanted the show to be relevant, to have something to say, albeit subtly, about the state of British society in the same way that the first series had.

'We felt very strongly, and so did Franc, that the series had to reflect the changes that had happened in British society in the past 15 years, rather than just thinking, "Let's get them in a hut." We knew we had to cover things like illegal labour and things like that, to show we were aware of the changes. To be fair, Franc and Jimmy did the homework for us there, and we had to catch up to make sure we weren't being naive, because we don't live in Britain any more."

Inspiration was initially easy to come by says La Frenais.

'The first episode had a clear brief: find out where they are, get them back together, outline the job, suck them in and they say yes. And that was easy. Then we started wondering what the fuck the second episode would be about [laughs]. We had a through line – that the bridge was going to be taken down and put up for the Indians. We didn't know how they were going to achieve it, though, when we started writing. Each episode just developed, as did the sub-plots.'

Once the first couple of scripts had been written and honed they were sent to the actors. Any doubts they may have had about the wisdom of reviving the show were erased once they started reading – certainly for Chris Fairbank.

'The script arrived and I remember not having the courage to read it for a bit. A couple of days, perhaps. I wondered if it would work. I opened it and page one, scene one it mentioned an Indian on a mountain, chanting. I thought, "What?" Then, it said, at the end of the chant he extends his arms outwards in a Christ-like pose and the scene dissolves to the Angel of the North and Dennis is driving a minicab. From that moment I thought it was brilliant and it just got better and better. I started reading it simply for pleasure. For me the scale, the ambition – it made other programmes seem like nothing, really. To be honest, apart from news and documentaries I don't watch much TV now. It's all, Grant from *EastEnders* as a prison officer, Grant from *EastEnders* as a policeman, all that sort of stuff. But this felt truly ground-breaking and the script stood up regardless of what had been made 20 years before.

'That said, I am the worst barometer for public opinion. If I think something is brilliant you can rest assured that everyone else thinks it is crap. I mean, I didn't think anyone else would want to watch 13 hours of stuff about hairy blokes on a building site. So I thought, "If I like it, then all the others will think it's rubbish." I was wrong. I was driving down the M4 to watch Wales play a World Cup qualifier against Poland when Jimmy called me and asked what I thought. I said, "I can't wait to start working on it." I think everyone felt the same.'

Kevin Whately, another who'd had misgivings, certainly did.

'As soon as I read the scripts I knew it would work. They are two very special writers and the scripts were as good as anything they've done. The shows were contemporary, relevant, and not just about a funny bunch of men on a building site.'

11: THE GOOD TIMES ROLL AROUND AGAIN

Noel Clarke was confused when he went to audition for the role of Wyman in the summer of 2001. He knew it was for a show called *Auf Wiedersehen, Pet,* but he could not believe it was an extension of the original programme. The only explanation was that it was a remake, an unimaginative, low-budget reprise with young actors playing the roles, perhaps being made for Sky One. At the audition he spoke to the director of the third series, Paul Seed.

'I asked him, "Are you casting new people for all the characters?" He looked at me as if I was mad. He said, "No, it's all the original actors. The only new one will be you if you get the part." A bead of sweat ran down my back. I don't usually get nervous before auditions, but when he told me that I got really nervous.'

Clarke was told the part was his on one condition: that he learned to drive. In one of the episodes set in Arizona, Wyman is run off the road by rednecks and this called for the character to drive a short distance. Clarke didn't have a licence. He was told to get one, so he took a two-week driving course, passed his test first time and was given the part of Wyman. He was delighted. When the first series was shown he might only have been eight, but he remembers watching it. 'I always remember Neville and Brenda being in bed,' he says now.

The series was by far the biggest production he'd taken part in. Clarke's acting break came when he was working at Kensington Leisure Centre and was spotted by a director, Ricky Beadle Blair, who was putting together a pilot for a show called *Heterosexuality*. He asked Clarke if he could act and then invited him to audition. He got the part and the show later turned into a programme called *Meterosexuality* and was shown on Channel 4. Nothing in his CV could have prepared Clarke for his role in *Auffpet*, though his natural confidence and belief in his ability meant he wasn't intimidated by the prospect.

He first met the cast during the read-through for the third series, held at St Mary's Abbot church hall, Kensington. Like most actors, Clarke has a morbid fear of being late, so he arrived at the venue before any other members of the cast. He didn't know what to expect.

'They had set up this ring of tables where the rest of the cast sat, apart from this table at the front facing them with seven chairs. That was for us seven. I sat down and there were six empty chairs beside me. I was thinking, "Oh man." I'm not one for being intimidated; after all, the likes of Jimmy Nail and Tim Spall are just people. I mean, what's the worst they could do? But I was a bit nervous, mainly about what they'd think of my performance. Especially someone like Tim Spall. What an actor he is. They'd been doing it for years so I was wondering if my performance would be up to the level required.

'Then they came in one by one and they were a really nice bunch of guys, and you could see they were all great mates. It must have been a bit shallow of me, but I always assumed Chris Fairbank was from Liverpool, but he came out with this really well-spoken, deep voice. I couldn't believe it. Instantly though they made me feel welcome and I relaxed a lot.'

It was August 2001 and Clarke wasn't the only new face to have been added to the core *Auffpet* group for the series. The BBC had decided not to hire the services of Roger Bamford, despite the fact that he was still working and many of the cast wanted him to be involved once more. Bamford claims he isn't too bothered by the decision, that he'd taken the show as far as it could go – though it rankles that no one from the BBC was willing to call him and explain that the programme was being revived but that they would be using another director. In his place they plumped for Paul Seed, who had directed high-profile series like *House of Cards*. *Doctor Who* fans will recognize him from his role as a villain in *The Ribos Operation*, back in 1978.

As well as the original six surviving members of the seven, there was one other *Auffpet* veteran in the third series: Julia Tobin. As mentioned earlier, she'd given up acting. However, as a friend of Whately's wife, Madelaine Newton, she'd heard rumours of a reunion – but never believed them to be true. Then Franc Roddam called her to see if she'd be interested in playing Brenda once more. She had no hesitation in saying yes. Revisiting Brenda, she says, was like 'seeing an old friend'. Tobin missed the read-through but met everyone at rehearsals.

'Ian La Frenais looked at me and said, "You haven't changed a bit!" I hadn't seen some of the guys for ages, but after a few minutes it was like we'd never been apart. It was so good to see

Previous page and opposite: New kid on the breeze-block, Noel Clarke, who was cast in the role of Wayne's son, Wyman.

them all. We really are like a family, and I feel like their sister.'

Chris Fairbank says the moment when the cast reunited to go through the scripts was a 'tingling' one.

'We sat around for a few days reading through the scripts, Dick and Ian pruning so that each episode fitted the time limit, checking that the lines fitted the characters. I remember thinking, as we sat there, that 16 years had just been edited out. It felt as if series two had finished on Friday and here we were on Monday starting the next series. I looked around at everyone, and I thought about how successful they had been over the years, yet here we were doing something that none of us thought would happen. It was a great feeling.'

There was a short break after the read-through followed by a week of rehearsals before shooting began in London. Tim Spall was completing a feature film and would not join the company until it relocated to Middlesbrough. For Noel Clarke, it was the first time he had acted on camera with the likes of Nail, Healy and Whately. Ironically, the group were filming around the conrner from where he grew up, at the Subterranean Club on Portobello Road in London, (doubling for Spennymoor in the northeast), shooting the scene in which Oz's son comes onstage in drag to sing a Dusty Springfield number. Clarke realized it was a different situation from the kind he was used to.

'Everyone had a seat with their name on it. They said, "Artist: Jimmy Nail" and "Artist: Kevin Whately". I didn't have one. I cracked a joke about it. Within 20 minutes this van pulled up, these guys got out and before I knew it there was a chair with my name on it. I was only kidding! I got really paranoid in case they all thought I was a bit of a diva.'

Those first few weeks of filming gave all concerned time to find their feet. For the main cast, it was the first time for more than 15 years that they had played their *Auffet* characters in front of camera. Tim Healy remembers it as a strange, uncertain period.

'I was involved on the first day of filming. I had to play a scene which wouldn't be shown until Episode 5, when Dennis comes back from Arizona to confront Bill Nighy's character. I'd never met Bill before in my life, never mind acted with him, and I'd not played my character for nearly 20 years and it felt weird. We played the scene and I was shite. Jimmy had done the same thing, played his first scene with Bill, and when I spoke to him on the phone he said the same: "I was crap!" We were thinking, "Who's Oz? Who's Dennis?" We couldn't find the characters.'

Whately had a similar experience. For the first three or four days he was filming scenes with Julia Tobin. But, despite her friendly, familiar face, he says it didn't feel as if they were shooting *Auffet*.

'Jimmy turned up on about the third day of filming and I was so pleased to see him, because until then it didn't feel right. Then a few of us filmed the scene when Oz's son comes out in drag and that felt much better.'

Once the production shifted to Middlesbrough the uncertainty decreased. However, it wasn't until Tim Spall arrived and all seven shot a scene with Ron Donachie's character Calhoun, in which he asks them about their knowledge of deconstructing and reconstructing bridges, that it

Oz (above) expected his son Rod (below) to be more Buffalo Springfield than Dusty Springfield.

felt as if the boys were back. Whately likens Spall's absence to a body missing a limb. Tim Healy says everyone felt complete.

'We did that scene and all of a sudden we just clicked back into it. We were like a football team passing the ball. Like Newcastle United. Well, Newcastle as they are now, not like they were 20 years ago. We felt, "We know who we are now. We might have been crap last week, but this week we're back on form." We all needed that scene. Those are the best in my eyes, when all seven of us are acting together. From that point on it was a doddle, a joy to do.'

Even the leaden skies of Middlesbrough failed to dampen people's enthusiasm. Chris Fairbank enjoyed every minute of it.

'It was cold, it was wet, it was miserable. There was the chemical factory belching out smoke everywhere. It was perfect, absolutely ideal and I mean that without a trace of irony. When Spall joined us it was a wonderful moment. Afterwards I remember that we all sat around, had a drink and we felt that the whole thing was working, that it was right. Not that it had been bad before then. Just that we'd been working in twos or threes and Spall was the final piece of the jigsaw.'

Life on location was no longer as carefree as it had been in either Germany or Spain. There was no willing sponsor to supply crates of Becks or San Miguel; given the age of most of the cast, Harvey's Bristol Cream might have been more suitable. Or Evian, given that a few of them have forsworn alcohol. But there was still time for enjoyment.

Noel Clarke had little trouble integrating himself. He says the other actors let him get on with his job and didn't try to bombard him with pearls of wisdom on the art of acting.

'They didn't give me any tips. The best tip I got was just watching them, seeing how they worked, that sort of thing. I said to them, "I'm not afraid to learn, so if you feel there is something I'm not doing then tell me."'

Chris Fairbank realized how hard it was for Clarke to fill the gigantic gap left by Holton, and how difficult it was for a young man to spend his days acting with 'us old farts'.

'I was acutely aware of the enormity of the pressure he was under, joining a show that started when he'd barely started school or something. I mean, we're all more than old enough to be his dad. He's young, single, ambitious and disgustingly good-looking, while we're all cynical, jaded actors who don't really have to work any more. I tried to make him feel part of it.'

Once filming in Middlesbrough had been completed, it was time to depart for Arizona. Shooting there had been jeopardized by the cataclysmic events of 11 September, and at one stage the production team had gone to Spain to find a location that could be used if getting to Arizona proved impossible. Thankfully, the problem became less critical and in late October the crew flew to Page, Arizona, via Phoenix. It was a flight Noel Clarke will always remember.

'I am not a good flier. At least, I'm all right once I'm on board. It's the thought of it I don't like. This was only a month and a half after 11 September so I was pretty scared. We landed in Phoenix and we had to get this tiny plane from Phoenix to Page over the Grand Canyon. I mean, it had propellers! Planes in this day and age shouldn't have those, man. The plane was rattling

Right: In fifteen years, Barry had gone from being a bewildered, boring Brummie to ... a wealthy, bewildered, boring Brummie.

and shaking and I really wasn't enjoying it. When we landed I said to the production people that I wasn't going back on that. When we finished five weeks later I got a lift back to Phoenix by road.'

Page County was no stranger to large television and film productions. Movies such as *Maverick* and *Evolution* had been filmed there; and, even more thrilling for some, so had a recent Britney Spears video. She'd even stayed at the Courtyard Marriott Hotel in Page, where the cast and crew were staying. This news helped to soothe Noel Clarke's troubled brow after his nerve-jangling fight across the Grand Canyon. 'I kept thinking: Please let her have stayed in my room,' he says.

The increase in airport security following 11 September was an inconvenience for one member of the cast. According to Whately, Chris Fairbank was always being stopped and searched at customs.

'Every time we went through an airport Chris was stopped by security. It was quite funny to begin with. Honestly, you'd be walking through and there'd be a beep and he'd be asked to step to one side. It got so that no-one wanted to go through security with him in case we got pulled too. It must be something in his eyes.' [Laughs]

Only a few months before, the makers of *The Planet of the Apes* had wrapped up their filming in Page. According to Fairbank, they had not made themselves popular with the locals, which meant the *Auf pet* crew were welcomed with open arms.

'Page is your original one-horse town. It came into existence in 1957 to house the workers who built the Lake Powell dam. All it has is a main street with a McDonald's, the Dam Bar and Grill, a small shopping mall and a Walmart where everyone ended up buying their low-caff, tall, skinny, vitamin-C-enriched lattes. The locals really took to us. *The Planet of the Apes* lot had been really rude apparently, yet here we were, the British Broadcasting Corporation, saying our "please and thank yous". It was a great experience. It knocked filming with Clint Eastwood in Zimbabwe, when Zimbabwe was a nice place to go, off the number one spot for my most enjoyable filming experience ever.'

On the first day of filming on the native American reservation the locals treated the cast and crew to a welcome dance. Healy says it was an amazing experience.

'They were dancing around going "Waaaiiiieeee, waaaaiiiieeee". Brilliant. I said to Jimmy, "Hey, it sounds like they're saying 'Why aye'." Jimmy passed that on to Mark Knopfler apparently and, I'm not sure, but that might have contributed to the song he wrote for the series: "Why Aye Man".'

The culture clash between the brickies and the native Americans wasn't confined to the storyline. Kevin Whately remembers one occasion – filming the meeting of the tribal elders – when art imitated life.

'Two of the guys didn't speak any English at all. All of the stage directions had to be translated for them. This meant they always reacted two seconds after everybody else. When we finished laughing they'd start. It threw the whole thing into chaos.

Above and below: Cowboys and Indians – the meeting of two great tribes.

Above: The Medicine Man, played by Saginaw Grant.
Below: Bill Nighy's portrayal of sleazy MP Jeffrey Grainger was one of the highlights of series three.

'Here's lookin' at yow kid.'

It sure beats Düsseldorf – cast members soak up the Arizona sun.

Dick Clement casts an authorial eye over filming of series three in Arizona.

Above: Chris Fairbank gets into character by pilfering a chair. Below: 'Tim, do you remember that time in Hamburg when ...'

Leader of the pack – Tim Healy's Dennis was still the gaffer.

Bomber offers a helping hand ... (above) ... while Oz elects to relax in the pool (below).

Above: Jimmy Nail with producer Joy Spink. Below: Lainie, played by Georgina Lightning.

Below: Chris Fairbank said filming the third series was the best acting experience he'd had since working with Clint Eastwood.

This page and left: Under the desert sun during the filming of the third series.

Above and below: Kevin Whately and Pat Roach run through a scene from the final episode.

'We were wetting ourselves, and the Navajos were wetting themselves. None of us had a clue what was happening. But some of those days were among the best I'd ever experienced: these amazing people, the sunsets, the colours, it was just fantastic. We had a ball.'

Noel Clarke considers himself privileged just to have been there.

'It was pretty intense but really enjoyable. When there was a break you could just sit outside the trailer and look at this deep blue sky and the red-rock canyons. You can't complain about that can you? Or you could speak to the native Americans and learn about them and their culture. They told us all about the struggle they'd faced to hold on to their heritage. Very few people get to speak to people like that and experience it, so I felt really lucky.'

Once the shoot in Arizona ended it was back to Bray Studios in Berkshire to film the rest of the show. In a nod to the first series, a hut was included – but it was set up in a warm, comfortable studio rather than on a freezing lot. Given that most of the cast were 20 years older than when Roger Bamford forced them to cram into an unheated, prefabricated one, this was probably wise.

The show then went into post-production, and the computer-generated graphics showing the Transporter Bridge being dismantled in Middlesbrough and the reconstructed one stretch across the Arizona desert were produced. The scene in which Oz, Dennis and Neville go to see Chip in Las Vegas was also constructed by the same special-effects team, Men from Mars.

A few changes were made during the editing process. Most significantly the original ending of the series was dropped. The plan had been that the lads would take a trip across the canyon on the bridge's gondola and that it would get stuck halfway, leaving them dangling there *à la The Italian Job*. But this didn't work and making it work would require a vast amount of computer-generated graphics, which in turn would stretch the show's budget beyond its means. Instead, a simple ending was chosen, in which all the lads except Bomber, who stays in Arizona to recuperate from illness, return to England.

The BBC announced that *Auf Wiedersehen, Pet* would return to British screens on Sunday 28 April 2002. A few traditionalists bemoaned the fact they hadn't stuck to the show's original time slot of Friday at 9 p.m., but the days when pubs empty for television shows have long since passed.

It would be fair to say that no one was certain how the public and the critics would greet this third series. News of *Auffet*'s revival had been met with a fair amount of publicity, and a few doubting voices had wondered at the pretty pass British television had come to if original programming meant rehashing 20-year-old series. Chris Fairbank was one cast member who was well aware of what the 'cynics' might say. He remembers attending the press launch for the BBC's spring schedule fully expecting to be ignored.

'We were in some faceless office block. There were people there from all the programmes that would be headlining the spring schedule and me, Pat and Kev, together with the press. They showed a video compilation of scenes from every programme. Before the credits had even finished, the *Auffet* table was swamped by every single journalist while the other tables had no one queuing behind them. It was kind of scary, embarrassing and thrilling at the same time. I was collared by some guy with a microphone and started an interview, when I was told by one of the producers to get back behind the desk because there were so many people waiting to ask questions. I couldn't get through the scrum, it was four or five people deep.

'But in a way that much interest was scary, because it meant the show's failure would be that much more public if it didn't find an audience. People were making very complimentary noises about the rushes, but then I've never been involved in a production yet when someone has said, "I have seen the rushes and I have to say, they are crap." That launch gave me an indication of the amount of interest and it panicked me, it really did. On the stage there is an element of control. You think, "If the Thursday night show goes bad, I can put it right on Friday." On TV you can't do that. You finish the job then it's all down to editors and directors. I think we were all a bit nervous about it.'

Dick Clement and Ian La Frenais arrived in Britain to publicize the show and were immediately give a foretaste of some people's cynicism. A local radio interviewer said to them, 'Aren't you flogging a dead horse?' Clement pointed out that they hadn't done the series because they were desperate for work. No one had in fact. They had done it because of the pleasure of working together once more, and in the belief that the British public wanted to see these much-loved characters once again.

Before the series was even aired, Franc Roddam was trying to get the BBC to commit to commissioning another one. His view was that by tying up the actors now they could get a better deal than they would after the show was aired and proved to be a big hit. He never countenanced failure. The BBC, however, was playing down expectations. The official screening the week before the first episode was broadcast was held in Newcastle. Tim Spall, Tim Healy and Jimmy Nail attended and saw that the response was reasonably positive. On the train back to London Franc Roddam was in first class with the Controller of BBC1, Lorraine Heggessy, and a few other BBC executives. Heggessy said she would be happy if the opening episode gained six million viewers. Executive producer Laura Mackie was keen to reach seven million. Roddam predicted nearer ten.

'I am an optimist and I was certain it would be a success. The two programmes that have continuously attracted huge viewing figures are *Coronation Street* and *EastEnders*. Why? Because they are shows about the working class. I told Lorraine and Laura that if we could get the people that watch those shows watching drama, watching this programme about people they recognize and with which they could associate their own lives, we'd get ten million people watching it. We knew there was an old audience for the show, the people who watched it when it was on. I suppose the question was if we could attract a new audience. I didn't see why not, and if we did then we'd get ten million people, easy. They all looked at me as if I was loopy.'

A good indication of what was to come occurred in February 2002, before the show was aired, when Whately, Nail and Healy returned to Newcastle city hall for another concert to raise money for the Sammy Johnson Memorial Fund. Once again the stalls were packed with *Auffpet* fans, who were aware that a new series was forthcoming and were eager to sample a taster for it. Clement and La Frenais had produced another two sketches for the three Geordies, filling in another part of their globetrotting past. It is entitled 'The Untold Story' and it is reproduced here for the first time:

DENNIS enters in working clothes, a can of Newcastle
Brown in his hand. He takes the applause and talks
directly to the audience.

DENNIS How are you? Good to see you back. Funny
thing happened to me and the lads a few years ago. No
one knows this story, 'cos we were forbidden to tell
it. When we came back from abroad these suits from
MI6 made us sign the Official Secrets Act. No,
seriously. We'd acquired highly sensitive information
and they wanted us to keep a lid on it. Said it was
in Britain's best interests. Well you've got to
respect the sanctity of the nation's security,
haven't you?

He shoots the audience a look — wouldn't you agree?

DENNIS Then the other day the Sunday Sun offered us
500 quid so we thought, bollocks, why not?

He takes a swig of his beer.

DENNIS It was 1990. I was the one heard about the gig
and had to talk the others into it...

A couple of chairs and an eye chart give the impression
of a doctor's waiting room. Neville is revealed,
looking nervous and worried. Dennis joins him.

NEVILLE What are all these shots for, Dennis?
DENNIS Hepatitis, A and B, typhoid, cholera and
dengue fever.
NEVILLE I can't believe you're taking us to a place
with all these diseases.

DENNIS Only a safeguard, man.
NEVILLE And are there lots of crawly things? Y'know,
like spiders and scorpions?
DENNIS Divvn't fret Nev, the snakes will take care
of those.

He chuckles. Neville doesn't.

OFFSTAGE A girl's voice:

GIRL (O.S.) Could you bend over that chair, Mr
Osborne?
OZ (O.S.) So tell me, nurse, can you look at a
person's bum and tell his character? I mean, you've
seen a few.
GIRL (O.S.) Too much fried food by the look of the
pimples.

Oz gives a long-drawn-out agonized yell. A moment
later the man himself appears, pulling up his
trousers. Neville looks alarmed.

NEVILLE You all right, Oz?
OZ As well as expected having just had a javelin
stuck up me arse! (He fastens his belt). Better be
worth it, Dennis.

All three guys pick up bags and walk downstage.
NEVILLE How do we get there?
DENNIS Newcastle to Heathrow, change at Frankfurt.
NEVILLE Long way from home.
DENNIS Howway, man, the wages are brilliant,
accommodation's top of the line. Three months in the
sun — what could be wrong with that?

A banner unfurls from the flies – an enormous propaganda picture of Saddam Hussein! Flight arrivals in Arabic and Arabic music. The lads register the picture, clutching passports and tickets.

OZ He must be the top banana.
NEVILLE Must be popular, his picture's everywhere.
OZ Reminds me of a foreman I worked with on a site at Peterlee. He was always smiling. Right bastard.
NEVILLE Looks a bit like Engelbert Humperdinck.
OZ Maybe it is. Always wondered what happened to him. Dropped out the charts and moved to Iraq.
DENNIS It's Saddam Hussein, you pair of hairbrains. It's his palace we'll be working on.
OZ Baghdad! It's got a ring to it, though but. The Thief of Baghdad. Ali Baba and flying carpets. Don't get that back home.
DENNIS Lucky to get flying linoleum in my street...

Dennis and Oz walk off into the dark. Neville takes a chair, scribbling on a pad of writing paper.

NEVILLE 'Dear Brenda, Well we're here, and it's stifling hot. Those shots must've worked though, I haven't caught anything yet. We're working on this gigantic palace. The labour force is from everywhere you can think of. Even a thousand Sudanese brickies, camped on the banks of the Tigris with only one bog between them. Hope they're not using the concrete mixers. Our digs are fine. And there's a few posh hotels with karaoke bars. The lads are happy, 'cos there's hundreds of sexually repressed Irish nurses...' No, I'd better not say that – shit!

He tears the page out and crumples it up. He gets up
as Dennis and Oz join him. In different shirts now,
for a night out. Disco music in the background. Oz
snaps his fingers, trying to get a barman's
attention.

OZ Three Heinekens here, effendi! And what do the
girls want?
DENNIS (to the barman) Vodka tonics, chief.
OZ Feisty little thing, that Siobhan. She spilt half
her drink down her cleavage, I said, 'Can I lick that
off?' She said, 'You can fuck off', I thought 'I'm all
right here.'
NEVILLE You should write a book on social etiquette, Oz.
OZ I've had offers.
DENNIS Her mate could be a goer an' all.
NEVILLE It's being Irish. They've thrown off the
shackles of the convent and they're rampant in the sun.
DENNIS (to Neville) How rampant's the one you were
chatting up?
NEVILLE I wasn't.
DENNIS Yes you were.
NEVILLE We were just talking music. I loaned her my
Best of the Smiths tape.
DENNIS Not a wise move, Nev. She listens to that
she'll hoy herself off the top of the nearest mosque.
IRISH VOICE (O.S.) Dying of thirst over here!
OZ Running all the way, pet! They walk offstage.

In the darkness we hear the sounds of the site.
Drills, hammers, shouts and Arabic music. FUAD walks
onstage, a dark-skinned Iraqi. He speaks reasonable
English in a thick accent.

FUAD Now you not work on site, you work down here only. Must finish very fast. Brick, plaster, tile, all of this.

The lads reappear in work clothes and hard hats. A heavy door closes behind them, cutting off the sounds of the site. They look around them curiously.

NEVILLE Why have we been moved?
FUAD Ask no question! Only tell what you need.
OZ How about a case of Newcastle Brown and three belly dancers?
FUAD No make joke. And you wear these always.

He hands them plastic laminated IDs and leaves. The lads pin them on.

NEVILLE Out the heat at least.
OZ Should be, we're at least three floors down.
NEVILLE What is this place? It's pretty luxurious. Look, there's a jacuzzi and a circular bed through here.
OZ Hugh Heffner would fancy this! Should get those Irish nurses down here, eh?
DENNIS Don't you realize where we are? Didn't you see that high-tech room when we got out the lift?
NEVILLE Aye. Looked like the flight deck of the starship Enterprise.
DENNIS This is not a Playboy mansion, lads. This is a military installation. We're working in Saddam Hussein's bunker!

Oz addresses the audience as Neville and Dennis leave.

OZ So... They kept us working in the bunker for 12-hour shifts. We flogged our bollocks off and it still wasn't fast enough for them. We realized why one hot night in August...

A rumbling sound is heard, growing louder.

OZ Thought it was an earthquake at first. Went out in the road and saw all these tanks and armoured cars heading south.

We hear a BBC voice:
BBC It's been confirmed that a massive force of tank-equipped Iraqi troops has moved into Kuwait City. Mrs Thatcher called President Bush and urged him to take a strong uncompromising stand...

We find Dennis and Neville 'at the bar' next to a good-looking woman called Lindsay. Oz joins them.

NEVILLE There's press and media all over the place. I've been trying to call Brenda but I can't get a line.
OZ Good job this, Dennis. Great pay, loads of OT. I hope this war won't bollocks it up for us.
DENNIS It will if the Yanks come after his arse and start bombing Baghdad.
NEVILLE What?!!
OZ Don't worry, Nev, we'll be all right in the bunker. Feet up on the vibrating bed, a kebab in the microwave and Godfathers I, II and III on the video.

Lindsay picks up on this. Her voice is American. Sexy, but with brains.

LINDSAY You guys work in a bunker?

OZ Aye, in the People's Palace.

LINDSAY What exactly do you do?

DENNIS We're brickies. That usually ends the conversation right there.

LINDSAY I thought a working-class hero was something to be.

DENNIS Aw, well if you're a John Lennon fan we might buy you a drink.

LINDSAY Vodka, straight. I'm Lindsay Heller.

NEVILLE Haven't we seen you on the telly?

LINDSAY I hope so. I'm with CNN. So what sort of stuff has Saddam got down there?

OZ What hasn't he got? It's a subterranean stag pad!

DENNIS (warningly) Oz!

OZ What?

DENNIS (to Lindsay) No offence, pet, but you're press and y'know, we're in a highly sensitive situation, like.

LINDSAY Sure, no sweat. Thanks for the drink.

They watch her legs as she walks away.

OZ Well I would, wouldn't you?

NEVILLE So you reckon we're in a scary situation, Dennis?

DENNIS No question. You don't piss around with these people. I heard a story from one of the pipe-fitters. Some minister disagreed with Saddam. Couple of days later his wife gets a parcel with her husband's head in it.

OZ Howway, man, Dennis, we're just brickies.

DENNIS Aye, but the three most strategically placed brickies in the whole of Baghdad!

As they walk off we hear a BBC Voice:

BBC Saddam Hussein added to the escalation of tension
in the Gulf by announcing that he intends to use
foreign workers as human shields...

The three lads enter 'the bunker', carrying their
tool kits.

NEVILLE What exactly is a human shield?
DENNIS It means using people like us to deter strikes
on military targets.
OZ They'll chain you to the front gate of a poison
gas factory, Nev. A prime target for allied aircraft.
And here they come! (RAF voice) 'Red Leader to Red
Two, moving in on target... I have visual contact...
target 400 yards... 200 yards... FUCK! It's
Neville!! Abort abort!!!

Dennis puts his fingers to his lips and hisses at
them to shut up.

DENNIS Keep it down, you dickhead! You can bet your
balls this place is bugged.
OZ But we're Geordies, no one can understand us!
DENNIS Just stick to the usual stuff, football and
sex.

The guys nod, 'got it'. Then:

OZ So, Nev, d'you poke that Lindsay?
NEVILLE Did I what?
OZ That's a sexual question! And she's been hurling
drinks down your neck the last few nights.

NEVILLE I'm married and that means something!
OZ Aye but no one would blame you. I mean, she's
gorgeous and she's on the telly.

Lights go down on the lads. Lindsay is revealed, a
stick mic in her hand:

LINDSAY Today was only the second time in the history
of the United Nations that members voted to use
military force. President Saddam's response was short
and sharp: 'If attacked we will never surrender.'
Lindsay Heller, CNN.

Lights go down on Lindsay and come up on Neville and
Dennis in the bunker again. They look up as Fuad
enters in a panic.
FUAD Out, out, quickly!
DENNIS We still have to plaster this wall —
FUAD Later, later! He is coming!
NEVILLE Who?
DENNIS Who d'you think?
FUAD Quickly! Must leave.

Fuad leaves, shouting commands to other people.

DENNIS Where's Oz?
NEVILLE He's in the bathroom. Been in there about
half an hour.
DENNIS What? Saddam Hussein's on his way and Oz is in
his bog!

BLACKOUT.

The Untold Story - Part Two

Lights come up on Oz, Neville and Dennis. Three
canvas chairs suggest their digs.

OZ So there I was, stretched out on the tiles, doing
a bit of plumbing. And suddenly I'm looking up at his
face. Him and all his generals.
NEVILLE Did he say owt?
OZ He muttered something to his entourage. I think
the gist of it was, 'Ask him where he gets his Doc
Martens'.
NEVILLE Bet it wasn't him. Bet it was one of his
doubles.
OZ What d'you mean, doubles?
NEVILLE He's got them all over the place, in case he
gets topped. Must come in quite handy, like. That way
he can open three hospitals and a shipyard all on the
same day.
OZ Bollocks - it was him! And you don't forget a look
like his. Dark and malevolent. A fearsome sight. Bit
like Graeme Souness moving in for the tackle.
DENNIS Wait a minute - what's this about doing a bit
of plumbing?
OZ I'd heard a rumour from the towelheads that he was
gonna come down. So I'd done a bypass on the pipes.
NEVILLE What for?
OZ I wanted a souvenir.

Oz picks up a carrier bag and pulls out a 16-ounce
jar that once contained pickled onions. Now something
long and dark floats in a colourless liquid. The
other two recoil.

DENNIS Is that what I think it is?
NEVILLE It is! It's a turd. That's disgusting!
OZ Not just any turd, lads. It's taken from the arse
of the Great Dictator himself.
DENNIS What are you gonna do with it?
OZ Take it back to Tyneside. Put it above the bar of
the Wallsend Working Men's Club.
DENNIS Have you not listened to a word I've said to
you the last few weeks? We're walking on eggshells
here. What d'you think they'd do to us if they found
out about this? Or do you want your head Fedexed back
to your granny in Gateshead?!

Neville walks forward as the lights go down on Dennis
and Oz.

NEVILLE They didn't find out, but we were still in
desperate shakes. Everyone else was shipping out –
builders, nurses. Embassies were closing. The French
were the first – not surprising. Oz went round there
and looted the kitchens. That night we had foie gras
and chips for our bait.

Dennis appears.

DENNIS We were still there through Christmas. And the
UN bombing deadline was getting nearer.
NEVILLE Brenda was frantic.
DENNIS And then Lindsay approached Oz. Said she
wanted to see all of us. In secret, like.

Oz and Lindsay join them.

NEVILLE So what's this about?

LINDSAY You guys will never make it out of here
without my help.
NEVILLE How's CNN going to help us?
LINDSAY In fact, I'm CIA.
The guys react in surprise.
OZ Aye, she's a spook.
LINDSAY We'll get you a vehicle. Maps, water, spare
gasoline. And a contact to get you to Jordan. But we
need something from you.
DENNIS What? A floor plan of the whole bunker?
LINDSAY He has bunkers all over Iraq, that's of no
particular interest to us.
DENNIS What then?
LINDSAY You have a stool sample.

The guys look at each other in surprise.

NEVILLE In God's name, what d'you want that for?
LINDSAY Medical analysis. It could tell the agency if
he's sick, dying, insane. Possibly all three.
DENNIS (to Oz) D'you still have it?
OZ I do.
DENNIS I told you to get rid of it.
OZ I didn't.
DENNIS Thank God for that.
NEVILLE How the hell did you hear about it?
LINDSAY We have our sources.
OZ I never said owt!
DENNIS Must've been a stool pigeon.
Lindsay leaves and the three Geordies address the
audience.

OZ We got out in the middle of the night just as the
first bombs started to fall.

THE GOOD TIMES ROLL AROUND AGAIN

NEVILLE We drove across the desert, got within a few
miles of Jordan, then almost got our arses shot off
by an SAS patrol.
DENNIS Bunch of Andy MacNabs pointing Armalites at
our heads.
OZ We said, 'Don't shoot, we're Geordies!' They said,
'What you doing out here?' I said, 'You go where the
work is, pal!'
DENNIS So that's it. That's the untold story.
NEVILLE Er... not quite.
DENNIS What do you mean?
NEVILLE There's something even you two don't know.
Something I've never told anybody.
OZ Are you queer, Nev?
NEVILLE It's more serious than that. That day when
Saddam came to the bunker...
DENNIS Aye.
NEVILLE Well soon as he'd gone I nipped into the
presidential bog. I know you told us we shouldn't,
Dennis, but when I have to go, I have to go.
OZ We all know that — where's this leading?
NEVILLE That wasn't Saddam's turd you hijacked, it
was mine!

Oz and Dennis react to this startling confession.

OZ You know what this means? Some top gun flew that
thing, packed in ice, on an air force jet to
Washington. And what did the lab boys find when they
put it under the scope? Saddam Hussein's system shows
dangerous levels of Newcastle Brown!

BLACKOUT.

12: THAT'S RELIVING ALRIGHT

Chris Fairbank admits he was concerned as Sunday 28 April drew closer. On the Friday before he was trying to calm his nerves, and catch up on the latest world events, by watching *Newsnight* on BBC2. As the closing credits rolled, Jeremy Paxman's voice gave way to the gentler tones of Mark Lawson, presenter of the *The Late Review*, in which three cultural critics shout at each other across a table about books, plays and films that few people have heard of, while Lawson nods his head vigorously and tries to get a word in edgeways. 'Coming up in the *The Late Review*,' Lawson's voice said over a soundless clip from the programme, 'a look at the new series of *Auf Wiedersehen, Pet*, a revival of a show that was successful 20 years ago. Is this the future of British television? Have things got so bad?'

'Oh God,' groaned Fairbank to himself, nursing his late-night cocoa. 'Can I bear to watch this?'

'The masochist in me said, "Yes". The critics were Germaine Greer, Tom Paulin and someone else I can't remember. It came round to the discussion and Mark Lawson said, "Have things got so bad, have ideas run out to such an extent that they have resorted to recycling old material?" I feared the worst. But it was remarkable. They showed a clip and it went to Tom

Paulin, who spends his time slagging off books and films by these respected writers and directors, and I thought he would bury it. But no, he loved it. [Adopting an intense Irish accent like Paulin] "It was just soooo good. These guys, these normal, working-class people, the kind of people who get shafted by life, yet they are still there with their heads held high. I thought it was just brilliant." I nearly stopped watching because it got so embarrassing. I was so relieved.'

Two days later the show went out. It was obvious from the start that many things were different. There was no pounding rock track sung by Joe Fagin to open it, an omission that left many fans disgruntled. (They should be consoled by the fact it might have been worse: Jimmy Nail might have been asked to sing.) Instead, a lonesome whistle plays over scenes of the sun-baked Grand Canyon while ghostly voices chant, 'Why Aye'. The opening shots were like those in a movie. The whole series was shot on film and so looked better, slicker than the first two. A first look at the characters showed they'd changed, grown older. Showing the Angel of the North, in both the opening and closing shots, gave another, more symbolic indication of the passing of time.

One thing remained the same: Dennis was still in the shit. At the start of the first series he, like all the others was forced to seek work abroad, but his downfall was given another dimension by his crumbling marriage. In the second series he was drinking too much, a result of being in hock to a local gangster. In the new series, 15 years on, life had become so bad that he had to resort to taxiing a drug dealer on his rounds for extra money.

Paulin was right: 15 years had passed and these men had slipped through the net. Neville was henpecked, 'running' a business, forever haunted by the taxman, a midlife crisis waiting to happen. In a memorable scene he and Dennis are at a garage when the latter castigates him for importing prefabricated homes for DIY freaks to put up at weekends, so putting honest artisans out of work. Neville counters fiercely. 'Artisans? Dinosaurs more like. This whole area used to be pit villages. Everybody worked for the colliery. You know what they do? All the men wear hairnets and pack airline meals. Everything's changed, Dennis. Deal with it.'

Almost two decades of social change are encapsulated in one image. Men who used to do the work of their fathers' down the mines – mines that provided whole communities with a focus and a purpose, the concept of communities – are reduced to pointless production-line work, packing food they'll never eat, dressed in clothes that make them all look the same. The scene and with Neville and Dennis is a terrific one, a sure sign that *Auf Pet* would still have something to say 20 years on. It might have had even more impact had it been shot, as was intended, at a factory near the town of Washington in Tyne & Wear that produces airline meals, but permission couldn't be obtained.

The rest of the characters are also in trouble. Moxey's working for a local gangster, desperately trying to going straight; Oz has done time in jail for cracking a few skulls while drunk; Bomber admits to doing only 'this 'n that'. Meanwhile, although Barry seems to have made good, it's only as a result of the black economy – he exports supermarket food past its sell-by date and unwittingly imports drugs from Russia. None of the characters can claim to be better off than they were the last time we saw them.

Right: The lads with Oz's new business partner, MP Jeffrey Grainger, on TV.

That's not to say the opening episode is bleak. Caustic, black humour punctuates the script. Discussing Oz's supposed death on the way to his funeral in Middlesbrough forces Dennis to ponder mortality. 'A terrible thing,' he tells Neville, 'when you look at the arc of a man's life and you see he was born in Newcastle and died in Middlesbrough.'

As a vehicle to draw the gang together, Oz's funeral is perfect, far more satisfactory than the way they were reunited in series two. Less than 20 minutes into the episode we realize his death was a ruse and the lads are reunited, Wyman completes the seven without too much effort. It also affords Jimmy Nail an unforgettable entrance, his tall, angular frame filling the doorway as the others discuss his death. We are also introduced to our bad guy, Jeffrey Grainger, the offspring of Jonathan Aitken and Jeffrey Archer after a night on the sleaze. We first see him during a louche TV interview in which he oozes insincerity about finding religion in prison, where Oz 'literally' saved his arse. Oz then outlines his outlandish plan to dismantle and sell the Transporter Bridge and the story is set in motion.

Tightly plotted, beautifully written and wonderfully acted, the show was a success. Seeing those characters and actors on screen was enough to remind you how pallid much TV drama, discounting the likes of *Clocking Off*, had become. It was a joy just finding out what had happened to them, seeing what had become of Oz, Neville, Dennis, Barry, Moxey and Bomber – even how Wayne had met his death – and reassuring to see they were all still fighting vainly against the bum hands they had been dealt.

The critics, who many thought were drooling in anticipation of giving a good mauling, were unanimous in their praise. In his review Jim Shelley of the *Daily Mirror*, failed to hide his disappointment that the show's quality had forced him to file his best barbs for another day.

'The public's appetite for nostalgia seems insatiable. Gareth Gates and Will Young are cheerfully massacring half the songs on their grannies' karaoke machines. ITV has brought back the BBC's *Forsyte Saga* and now the Beeb has updated ITV's *Auf Wiedersehen, Pet*. This looks complacent and that they've run out of ideas but surprisingly they've done a good job... With Jimmy Nail's mugging for the camera kept to a minimum, the real star was the writing with Hollywood exiles Ian La Frenais and Dick Clement at their sharpest, especially about the North East.'

The *Times*'s Paul Hoggart made the point that because characters were interesting to begin with, they still remained so, especially with the actors taking to their roles 'like ducks to Newcastle Brown'.

'Since this is the first, middle and last requirement of good television drama, it is an auspicious start... The sharp writing and dry humour spice what is, underneath, as bleak as any heavy, social issue based drama. It's just a lot more fun to watch.'

James Walton of the *Daily Telegraph* said it was superbly acted and likeable but not up there with Clement and La Frenais' best. The *Daily Mail*'s Christopher Matthew was more effusive, even breaking his newspaper's purdah on praising Greg Dyke's BBC.

'All credit to Tim Healy, Timothy Spall, Christopher Fairbank, Kevin Whately, Jimmy Nail and Pat Roach for hurdling the age gap with such aplomb. And Dick Clement and Ian La Frenais for a delightful script that was as fresh and as funny as ever, and to the BBC drama department for a leap of imagination unparalleled in living memory. Despite the sad loss of Gary Holton as

Wayne, last night's episode was an unalloyed pleasure – funny, touching, utterly believable and brilliantly acted by one and all.'

Over on the *Daily Express*, Robert Gore Langton was dusting off his superlatives.

'The meat of the show is not just in the sharpness of the writing and its flashes of social realism, but also in the effortless confidence of the cast. Everything from Chris Fairbank's Moxey ("I'm not stupid, just strange") to Jimmy Nail's underpants seemed a treat. There's a long way to go, but for an opener this was terrific. The new *Auf Pet* already has 'vintage' stamped all over it.'

More important than the reaction of the critics was that of the public. In this respect everyone's expectations were exceeded. The next day unofficial overnight viewing figures estimated that 11.6 million people had watched the episode, a staggering 46 per cent share of the audience. This was in a time slot where the BBC had been losing out to ITV for months, years even. The previous week another drama-comedy *Rescue Me*, had been watched by only 3 million viewers. Ironically, on the other side ITV were showing a remake of another television classic, *The Forsyte Saga*, but its audience withered away. The only BBC dramas or comedies that had gained more than 10 million viewers in the preceding months were old reliables like *EastEnders*, *Casualty* and the Christmas special of *Only Fools and Horses*. The BBC were jubilant – the gamble had worked.

Why did people still feel such an affinity for the show? It has to be the characters. The mix of personalities and the ensemble that play them somehow touches a chord with the British public. People love to look back, to revisit old friends and catch up on what they are doing. That might explain the success of Friends Reunited. Though it still doesn't explain or excuse why anyone brought back *Crossroads*.

Franc Roddam believes it's because people can judge the changes in their own lives against those of the characters in *Auf Pet*. He may be right. Or it could simply be because viewers are starved of dramas with well-drawn, recognizable characters they can care about and empathize with, with a few sharp lines thrown in as garnish. Whatever the reason, the show's instant success both surprised and delighted its veteran writers. La Frenais says it gave them both 'enormous pleasure'.

'It was the first bit of British TV we had done for a long time, a decade or so I think. It was great to write a one-hour drama series, especially after all the frustrations of working in the movies, when you can write two or three years before anything actually happens. When we all met for that lunch at the Mirabelle, Dick and I had three movie projects on the go, two of them with directors attached and one with a star. From that lunch to the series being screened all those movie projects had barely moved an inch. So it was nice to write something and then see it on screen almost straight away. And it was very sweet that it was such a success.'

None of the actors could believe it. Julia Tobin realized she was involved in something big once more when people started smiling at her in supermarkets, rather than ignoring her as they do the rest of us. The cast phoned each other in disbelief. They had all hoped that the series would be welcomed, but none had thought the welcome would be so warm. Noel Clarke was in HMV when a punter came across to him. 'Your dad would be proud of you,' the man said. Clarke smiled indulgently. 'Yes,' the guy added, 'old Wayne would be pleased as punch at you.'

Nevenda Homes' secretary, Lorraine, (right) caught Neville's wandering eyes and created tension with the formidable Brenda (above and bel...

Moxey (right and page 179) was forced to do one of his many runners after stitching up Mickey Startup, played by Michael Angelis (below and next page).

A bridge too far? The lads plan their biggest job yet, taking down the Transporter Bridge.

The project was unpopular with both the locals (below right) and the Serbian and Bosnian workforce, led by Yorgo (above, and above right).

Once a radish always a radish – both his wife Tatiana, and Jeffrey Grainger run rings around poor old Barry.

Oz struggles to come to terms with the sexuality of his son, Rod, played by Mark Stobbart.

Joe Saugus, played by Gordon Tootoosis

Where's Barry? Oz and the gang experience some good old-fashioned American justice after drugs are found in Barry's baggage.

Courtroom drama – Barry was up before the bench while the rest of the gang sweat it out in the jailhouse.

Grafting in the desert sun is thirsty work.

A long way from Düsseldorf – the lads sweat in the Arizona heat.

Left and below right: The lads, led by Dennis, help sort out Barry's love life, and being double-crossed by Grainger (above right).

Clark nodded. 'You do know that he's not my real dad, don't you?' he said. The man nodded. 'Yeah, but he'd be so proud of you.'

As soon as the BBC saw the viewing figures they decided to try and retain everyone's services for another series. Meanwhile, *Auf pet* held its audience, with the figures never dipping below 10.5 million. Although the show was unable to sustain the stunning quality of its first episode, that made the remaining five shows very good at worst, and excellent at best.

There are a few flaws. Bomber never really gets much to do – again. And, not that any fault can be found with Noel Clarke, who turns in an excellent performance, Wyman's character appears underdeveloped, and the reason for his being in Arizona seems a bit tenuous given that he knows nothing about the construction industry. A scene in which he asks Dennis if it's OK if he tags along to Arizona was cut from the show. ('Why aye, man, Wyman, man,' Dennis replies, to the young man's bewilderment.) His abrasive relationship with Oz never fully convinces, and more could perhaps have been made of that. And the sub-plot of Oz foisting his ponderous, dull Dire Straits dad rock on to Wyman is absurd. (Might it not have worked better the opposite way around, with Wyman persuading Oz of the merits of speed garage?) And there are several times when this viewer wanted to see more of old, obnoxious, abusive, surly Oz, rather than the sober, slim, suit-wearing modern version.

Those are minor quibbles, however. On the whole the series was a triumph from start to rewritten finish. Some people argued that the entire plot was too far-fetched, but to criticize a show for being ambitious is miserly. As both the writers and the actors have pointed out, to have

DI Harteley (far left) joins Joe and the gang to watch a traditional native American dance – and watch Grainger go up in smoke.

set the series on a building site near Ponteland would have been a step back, a sure sign that the characters had neither changed nor developed in the course of two decades. An indication of this was when the writers contrived to have the characters sharing a hut in the desert, to re-create their days of confinement in Germany. It didn't quite work as most of the main characters were less antisocial in their habits and everyone knew each other well.

The sub-plot that involved Barry's wife and her shady Russian 'brother' deceiving him worked well. Everyone – viewers and the other characters – knew he was being a 'radish'. That Barry had transformed himself into a ruthless, successful businessman would have been a change too great to swallow. But Tim Spall's portrayal of a man desperately trying to cling on to an illusion in the face of mounting evidence, and his humiliation when it became palpably clear he'd been duped, was superb. As was Branka Katic's performance as his purring, pouting wife Tatiana, perhaps the reason why her character has been chosen to appear in the next series.

It was also a pleasure to see Chris Fairbank's Moxey given a meatier role than in the previous two series. That was done deliberately, Ian La Frenais says, a sort of redress for past scripts when his role was sketchy at best. Bill Nighy's rather camp but hilarious turn as the scheming, shifty Tory, Jeffrey Grainger, his voice as rich as a chocolate and foie gras smoothie, is an *Auf pet* rogue to rank alongside Ally Fraser. Once again Oz gets to seduce the gangster's moll, this time a pinstriped Sloane played by Emily Bruni rather than the tarty Geordie Lesley St John portrayed so memorably in the second series. Yet another sign of Oz's upward mobility.

The series had such an impact on the public that there were people who believed elements of the plot to be true. Middlesbrough Council had to issue a press release assuring the town's inhabitants that the Transporter Bridge was not being taken down bit by bit, that what they were seeing on screen was an effect achieved by computer-generated graphics – a testament to the convincing work done by Men from Mars. It was so realistic that one couple reportedly travelled from Portsmouth for a last look at the bridge. To back up the council's press release, the *Sun* public-spiritedly dispatched a bus of Page Three girls to Middlesbrough to be photographed in front of the bridge and prove it was still there.

The most virulent criticisms offered on Internet message boards and in the chat rooms where *Aufpet* fanatics gathered was of the theme music. The question was: where was Joe Fagin? The author tried to locate him but failed. Whether the release of a greatest hits compilation in May 2002 was entirely coincidental, given the start of the third series, is uncertain. Fagin was last heard of playing a concert in the Middle East – the organizers allegedly believed they were going to get Donald Fagin, of jazzy pop duo Steely Dan. Not everyone missed Fagin. In fact, his voice over a middle-of the-road rock backing would surely have dated the show immediately. For the third series, viewers were treated to Mark Knopfler's 'Why Aye Man', with backing shouting from Tim Healy and Jimmy Nail. Only the chorus was used, but the lyrics of the song refer to the first series, to men forced by the policies of Mrs Thatcher to leave their homes and find work in Germany. 'Nae more work on Maggie's farm, haddaway down the Autobahn, Mine's a Portakabin bed, Or a bunk in a Nissen hut instead,' Knopfler sings in the full version. Not quite 'A pint with the boys in a bar full of noise,' but almost.

On Sunday 2 June the series came to an end. But this time it was only a couple of months before there was another, minor cast reunion, this time to film a sketch for *Comic Relief*, to be broadcast on Friday 14 March 2003. Written by Clement and La Frenais, and featuring Healy, Nail, Fairbank and Whately, the sketch was shot at the Dorchester on Park Lane, London and at the Clarence Hotel in Dublin, owned by U2 whose lead singer, Bono, made a cameo appearance. The sketch is printed here.

```
Fade in: Int. Hotel Lobby (Miami) Day

Chaos and confusion. The lobby is crowded with people,
most of whom are in line at the check-in, trying to get
a room. Piles of luggage and more being wheeled in by
staff. We discover NEVILLE HOPE, trying to find a quiet
corner as he talks into his mobile.

NEVILLE Brenda? Hello, pet, it's me... No we're still in
Miami, most of the flights have been cancelled... Oh it
was a full-scale code-red terrorist alert at the airport,
but I don't want you to worry...
```

More baggage is wheeled in from the street. Oz is revealed with Moxey.

OZ There's our kit, Mox — grab it!
MOXEY Right!

Oz joins Dennis at the counter where DOLORES, a pretty Hispanic desk clerk, is hitting keys on the computer.

OZ What's the story then?
DENNIS She's checking the computer but she very much doubts it.
OZ No beds in a place this size?
DENNIS All these unexpected bookings, isn't it? Look around you, it's lunacy.

Moxey hauls bags off the luggage cart. He has a pile of three, including a backpack and a Newcastle United shoulder bag. He grabs a grey Samsonite case and puts it with the pile. Then notices he already has a grey Samsonite. Odd. He clicks it open. His eyes widen. He's looking at stacks and stacks of used dollar bills. Hundred dollar bills... He stares at them, then closes the case — and puts the other bag back on the cart. RESUME Dennis and Oz, talking to Dolores.

DOLORES I'm sorry. I suggest you try the Marriott.
OZ Listen, our flight to the UK's been cancelled. Before that we sat on the tarmac in Caracas for four hours. That's in Venezuela.
DOLORES That is my country. Very beautiful.
OZ It might be beautiful if you're sitting on a beach with a pina colada, pet. Not when you're building a

sewage reclamation plant on the mouth of the Orinoco for three months.

DENNIS On top of that, rebels took our gaffer hostage, so we didn't get paid. We're desperate for a little R & R. No more than we deserve.

DOLORES I'd like to help but is not possible.

MOXEY (joining them) Any luck?

OZ Not yet.

DOLORES The only room we have is the honeymoon suite. Twenty-three-hundred dollar a night, plus tax.

Dennis and Oz raise their eyes — no way.

MOXEY We'll take it.

He plonks down a bundle of notes on the desk. INT. HONEYMOON SUITE (MIAMI) DAY. An ASSTANT MANAGER shows them into a luxurious open-plan suite. Moxey clutches the case — the others only have their duty-free bags. The centrepiece is an enormous circular bed with an overhead mirror. Exotic flowers, a fruit basket — at these prices, they get the full treatment.

MANAGER Fully stocked minibar, cable TV, jacuzzi and mood lighting. There should be everything you need, gentlemen.

OZ Hey, don't get the wrong idea, amigo! This is the only room you had. We're not here for some brickies' gang bang.

NEVILLE (embarrassed) Thank you very much, it will do very nicely.

MANAGER The rest of your luggage should be up at any moment.

He leaves. Only now they're alone can they ask questions.

DENNIS Did you have that cash tucked away somewhere, Mox? 'Cos you borrowed 50 bucks off me in Caracas.
MOXEY You could say I had a little windfall.
OZ What wind was this?

Moxey slings the suitcase on the bed.

MOXEY This case. It isn't mine. It looks like mine, but it isn't.
NEVILLE What do you mean? I put me hairdryer in your case.
MOXEY I'll buy you a new one.

He clicks it open. They all stare at the money.

OZ Bloody hell's bollocks!
NEVILLE How much is in there?!
MOXEY I haven't counted it.
DENNIS They're all hundreds! Could be two, three million dollars.
NEVILLE But it's not yours, you've got to give it back. Some bloke in this hotel is three million dollars short! And he won't be content with my hairdryer and 12 pairs of dirty underpants.
MOXEY This money's dirty, Nev.
NEVILLE How d'you mean?
MOXEY Must be, mustn't it? Legit people don't carry around this much cash.
OZ He's right. Look where we are — Miami. Everything comes through here. Drug money, mob money, arms money.
NEVILLE Oh that's comforting! And you think they won't come looking?

A knock on the door. They freeze, almost peeing themselves.

DENNIS Who is it?
BELL CAPTAIN (V.O.) Bell captain, sir.

Moxey closes the case. Dennis opens the door. The bell captain wheels in the rest of their bags.

DENNIS Thanks very much, just leave them there, we'll take care of it.
MOXEY Here!

He tips him. The bell captain pockets the 100 dollar bill. His attitude is instantly ingratiating.

BELL CAPTAIN Thank you, gentlemen. I'm Phil. Anything you need, just ask for Phil.
OZ Four cheeseburgers, chips and two bottles of Dom Perignon.
MOXEY I'd like mine well done.
OZ And extra pickles.
BELL CAPTAIN You got it!

He goes. Dennis waits until the door has closed.

DENNIS Are you both off your trolley? You're spending the money as if it's ours — it's not!
MOXEY No one's gonna report this, lads.
OZ Moxey's right! This is dirty money. Soiled, grubby, filthy — and it's ours!
NEVILLE It's not! It belongs to bad, evil people who'll hunt us down and... and chop bits off us!
OZ We'll be out of here in the morning, won't we? Back home. Columbian drug barons aren't gonna hunt you down in Gateshead. Anyhow, this is a spit in the ocean to them.
DENNIS What if it's the Mafia? Or worse, the Russian

Mafia? Or worse, the Jamaican yardies.
MOXEY Oh they are evil, I've heard that.
NEVILLE What if they're Albanian Mafia? They'll cut our throats, disembowel us and then ask us where the money is.
OZ Lads, lads - pull yourselves together. No one knows where this case is. And as Moxey says, no one can report it. This is a gift from the Big Brickie in the sky. To make up for all the shite we've been through. And over the years we've been through a lot of shite.

This at least makes Neville and Dennis think about it.

NEVILLE I suppose I could pay off the VAT.
OZ Yes you could, Nev. I think I'd sooner get a pair of high-class tarts up here and shag them in the jaccuzi.
MOXEY An Aston-Martin and a hair transplant for me.

Dennis isn't buying this.

DENNIS Wait a minute! You've got to think this through. What if we did take the money home? What are we gonna do with it? Am I gonna walk into the Abbey National and tell the manager to put half a million on deposit? 'Had a great day at Kempton Park, Mr Treadaway.'
MOXEY Bury it. In a shoebox.
OZ And lose the interest? Look, there are banks that don't ask any questions. Where d'you think those bent bastards from Enron bunged their wonga?
MOXEY Yeah, we'll open an account in the Bahamas or the Cayman Islands. Somewhere we can snorkel when we visit our money.

Another knock on the door. Again, they freeze in fright.

DENNIS (a whisper) Don't open it.
OZ Divvn't panic, Den. Probably room service.
NEVILLE Can't be. Not this quick. Four cheeseburgers? And Moxey's was well done.

Moxey puts the case under the bed. Oz opens the door. FRANK has a hard look. Not the kind of guy you'd mess with. He wears a dark suit and a T-shirt. American accent.

OZ Who are you?
FRANK Who am I? I'm Frank, who are you?
OZ Oz.

The guy looks round the others.

FRANK Someone here called Moxey?
MOXEY Could be.
FRANK I got a case belongs to you.
MOXEY How can you be sure it's mine?
FRANK Some pills inside. Name on the label is Moxey.
MOXEY Oh for my hay fever, yeah.
FRANK I checked with the front desk, they said try the honeymoon suite. (He looks at each of them.) Who's the bride?

Neville looks faint. Frank stares at him.

FRANK (cont'd) You OK? You look pale.
NEVILLE Me, no I'm just a bit queasy from the flight. Shouldn't have had the shrimp.
MOXEY Well thanks very much. I'll come and get the case, shall I?
FRANK I don't suppose you inadvertently took a similar case belonging to my people.

DENNIS Who are your people?
FRANK You know who we are.

The guys are frozen with indecision.

FRANK (cont'd) OK, I don't want to be dicked around.
Let's say you find the case. Bring it to the penthouse.
In five minutes.

He leaves. The guys are silent for a moment. Neville
needs to sit down.

NEVILLE What did he mean by 'You know who we are'?
DENNIS Obvious, isn't it? They're hard-core mobsters.
Moxey, get the case and take it back.
MOXEY Me?
DENNIS You got us into this.
MOXEY You heard what he said. Penthouse! I give them the
money and you'll see me hurtling past this window in two
minutes.
OZ We'll go team-handed. They're not gonna hoy four of
us off.
NEVILLE Could I just call Brenda first?
INT. CORRIDOR HOTEL DAY
The guys ring the doorbell of the penthouse. They wait,
apprehensive and dry-mouthed. The door is opened by
Frank. He registers the case and nods 'Come in'. They
step over the threshold.

INT. PENTHOUSE SUITE DAY
Frank closes the door behind them and the guys step into
the room. They react in astonishment. They're not facing
the Sopranos – it's Bono and Larry from U2, sprawled
around with drinks, magazines and guitars. Wordlessly,

Bono gets up, takes Moxey's case and puts it on the table.
Then he hands him the other case. Both cases are opened,
the lads on one side, Bono, Larry and Frank on the other.
Bono nods to Moxey.

BONO You got a hat just like The Edge.
MOXEY Yeah. But I got mine at Oxfam. His was probably
handwoven by virgins in Tipperary.
BONO County Kerry.
FRANK Everything there?
NEVILLE Looks like it. Got me hairdryer.
DENNIS You might be a bit short. We paid cash for the
room, like.
BONO Have it on us.

The guys react in relief and gratitude.

OZ Aw, cheers. Any chance of tickets for your show
tonight?
LARRY (to Bono) Why not?
OZ Backstage passes?
BONO (with sarcasm) D'you want a ride in our customized
Gulfstream as well?
OZ No thanks, we'd miss out on the air miles.

Frank closes the case — the business is done.

DENNIS Lot of readies to carry around with you, lads.
FRANK On the road, a lot of promoters prefer paying cash.
BONO Anyway this is going to charity. Comic Relief.

Larry and Frank react in surprise.

LARRY Since when?

FRANK What all of it?
BONO Didn't I mention this?
LARRY Did you bollocks! Do The Edge and Adam know about this?
BONO They'll be cool.
LARRY You don't know that - Jaysis.
FRANK Maybe you guys should discuss this later.

He indicates for our guys to get lost. They tactfully start to leave.

BONO It's for a good cause, y'know?
LARRY Yeah, but I thought we were saving up to buy Andorra.

INT. CORRIDOR HOTEL DAY
The door closes on the argument.

NEVILLE All that money! And they're just gonna give it away.
MOXEY Maybe that's what we should all have done.
DENNIS What?
MOXEY Been a band, instead of brickies.
OZ Well it's not too late...

They walk off down the corridor, singing in unison:

ALL 'In the name of love...'
(Or whatever song they think is appropriate...)

13: AND THERE WE WERE, AND HERE WE ARE

Before the third series had ended, discussions about making another one were already under way. Ian La Frenais had the idea of setting it in Cuba, while at the hotel bar during the filming of the third series.

'We'd decided that having gone to the trouble of getting us all together again, we should do another series. Someone mentioned Australia. Apparently the BBC has some deal there; you can get tax breaks if you film there or something like that. I thought, "What's different about Australia? There's no cultural shock; they're not fish out of water there." Cuba appealed; Cuba's sexy, the palm trees, the music, the faded glamour. Everyone loved the idea. Even before the third series had been screened, Jimmy, Franc, Dick and I had been there on a recce and got loads of ideas. It was while we were in Cuba that we discovered there was a special department in the Foreign Office that employs building companies to work exclusively on British government buildings, for security reasons. Any rebuilding has to be done by the Brits. When we found that out, Dick and I thought, "It's the dream job for the boys."'

The script for the fourth series adapts the idea that never really was, that came to Clement and La Frenais when they saw British builders renovating the British Embassy in Prague. The plan then had been to place the lads in Moscow during the cold war but when this ended the concept was dated. Then came the idea of setting the series in Cuba, one of the few Communist countries left.

Unfortunately, Fidel Castro refused to grant permission for the cast and crew to shoot in the country. So the neighbouring Dominican Republic was selected as a substitute. However, at the time of writing, immediately prior to the series going into production, the team were still hoping to be given permission to film some scenes in Cuba.

On 14 April, 2003, a week before leaving for Central America, the cast gathered for a read-through of the fourth series at the Brompton Oratory in South Kensington in London. As the actors greeted each other warmly in the spring sunshine it was easy to see how unique a series *Auf pet* is. No other production has been away from the screen so long and been revived so successfully. And no other programme has forged a cast whose members are as good friends off screen as they are on. The only other show with such a large group of principal characters who have entered the national consciousness and are held in deep affection is *Dad's Army*. And even it had its problems, famously when Arthur Lowe stipulated in his contract that on no account would he perform a scene in which his trousers fell down. Most other long-running shows develop problems, with personality clashes and petty rivalries. This is what Chris Fairbank has to say about his fellow actors in *Auf pet*.

'Of course we've had our differences but nothing major. We've always had a laugh. It's all down to the strength of the material. If you have a terrific character with wonderful lines then you don't need to try and change things or bring attention to yourself. There was an extraordinary generosity at the start of that third series. There were several times when there was a cracking line attributed to one character when we thought, "Actually that might be better said by Bomber," or "That line of Moxey's is better suited to Oz" and you just hand it over. That really doesn't happen in other shows as far as I'm aware. It's easy to get toe-curlingly soppy about it, but the collective focus is what's best for the show; that's the star, not any of the individuals.

'This show was the big break for all of us and we went through a lot together. The huge success of that first series changed many of the guys' lives and that was something we spoke about. Then all the hassles of the second series and, of course, Gary's death, which was awful, yet brought us together even more. We're a group … gang if you like.'

Just like the characters they play on screen – although, of course, the actors are nothing like the people they portray. But, like the lads, they are all different personalities, and each has their role in the group. Julia Tobin says this of them:

'Chris Fairbank is a great raconteur, full of stories; Tim Spall is much quieter but very funny and a superb actor; Tim Healy is the comic, he has a very dry wit; Kev is really down to earth, just a pleasant, helpful man; Pat is massive in size compared to me. He's a real gentleman; he never swears in front of women and he always takes care of me wherever I am. Jimmy is lovely; a wonderful, charming bloke.'

According to Noel Clarke, the actors, like their characters, are wont to reminisce about times past over a pint or, as is more common now, a bottle of mineral water.

'Something will happen and one of them will turn to the rest and say, "Remember when we were in Germany and …", or "What about that time in Spain …" You can tell they are great mates. They seem to enjoy each other's success and that is a rare thing in this industry.'

An expected offshoot of the third series' success was a rekindling of press interest in the main actors. Inevitably, mischief-making stories about rows over pay appeared in some newspapers, all of which are strenuously denied by members of the cast. There were a few doubts about the viability of a fourth series, but these were assuaged once the scripts arrived. Chris Fairbank describes them as among the best he's ever read. Tim Healy, too. The question most fans want answered is: how long can they go on? Healy believes the next series might be the last, excluding a one-off special. Who knows? As he admits, when it comes to *Auffpet* it pays to never say never.

EPISODE GUIDE

SERIES ONE
Broadcast 11 November 1983
to 14 February 1984

SERIES TWO
Broadcast 21 February 1986
to 16 May 1986

SERIES THREE
Broadcast 28 April 2002
to 2 June 2002

SERIES ONE

PRINCIPAL CAST

Tim Healy: Dennis Patterson
Kevin Whately: Neville Hope
Jimmy Nail: Leonard 'Oz' Osbourne
Timothy Spall: Barry Taylor
Gary Holton: Wayne Winston Norris
Pat Roach: 'Bomber' Busbridge
Chris Fairbank: Albert Arthur 'Moxey' Moxall
(From episode two)

OTHER MAIN CAST

Julia Tobin: Brenda Hope
Michael Sheard: Herr Grunwald
Peter Birch: Herr Ulrich
Brigitte Kahn: Dagmar
Ray Knight: Barman
Lysette Anthony: Christa
Michael Elphick: McGowan
Ray Winstone: Colin
Caroline Hutchinson: Vera Patterson
Su Elliott: Marjorie Osbourne
Lucinda Edmonds: Tracey Busbridge
Lex van Delden: Helmut
Christine Garner: Ingrid
Berwick Kaler: Alan
Oona Kirsch: Heidi
Des Young: Hedley Irwin

01: IF I WERE A CARPENTER

First broadcast: 11 November 1983

Oz, Neville and Dennis escape Newcastle for their own reasons: Dennis to escape from his failing business and marriage; Neville to earn money for a new home for him self and Brenda; Oz to get legless. The three travel to Germany where they get work in Düsseldorf, though Neville has to pose as a carpenter. Once at the site the lads find themselves living in a hut with a lecherous Cockney, a boring Brummie, and a West Country giant. The gang visit a brothel where Neville gets a tattoo that thwarts his plans to return home.

02: WHO WON THE WAR ANYWAY?

First broadcast: 18 November 1983

Moxey makes his entrance. Neville's lack of carpentry skills continues to put his digits in danger. Meanwhile, Oz attempts to start World War III with the Germans and is fired after starting a fight in bar. Neville gets his job. Oz is recalled and is prevented at the last minute from travelling home. Dennis suggests a game of darts against the Germans as a reconciliatory gesture, to which Oz agrees – though he points out, 'They're still the bastards that bombed me granny.'

03: THE GIRLS THEY LEFT BEHIND

First broadcast: 25 November 1983

Mrs Osbourne tracks Oz down via Vera, demanding to know where her errant husband is. For some reason the Geordies go to support Sunderland in Europe and Oz, after a night on the Pils, ends up on a flight back to the northeast, where he has a less than romantic reunion with Marjorie. The lads, believing he has gone for good, auction off his stuff and send the proceeds back to Tyneside. Oz returns and is none too pleased when he hears of this. 'I'm sure your wife will find a use for it,' Neville says helpfully.

04: SUSPICION

First broadcast: 2 December 1983

Property goes missing from the hut and the finger of blame is pointed all around. Various plots are hatched to catch the culprit, all of which fail. It turns out the thief is not one of our lads.

05: HOME THOUGHTS FROM ABROAD

First broadcast: 9 December 1983

We get to meet Mrs Bomber when word reaches Germany that one of Busbridge's daughters has run away from home. While he travels back to England, she turns up in Dusseldorf sporting a pretty face and a rather ropy West Country accent. The former means that few of the lads trust her in Wayne's company, though he tries manfully to repel her advances. Bomber returns and all ends well. Neville's part-time job is revealed to be as an Indian waiter, while Barry and Moxey indulge their creative sides by planting a small herb garden.

06: THE ACCUSED

First broadcast: 16 December 1983

Diplomatic relations between the English and the Germans are reduced to rubble because of Oz's yobbery. They worsen when Nev, whose luck with women has never been anything other than dire, is accused of assaulting a German girl who shares a taxi home with him. Brenda makes a trip out to Germany, Dennis takes control and Neville is finally released by the police when the Germans rally round to help catch the real culprit.

07: PRIVATE LIVES

First broadcast: 30 December 1983

Poor old Dennis seeks to extricate himself from the group and spend a romantic evening with Dagmar. Matters of romance are also on Barry's mind and he seeks Wayne's advice on how to strike up relations with the opposite sex. They tail two Swedish air hostesses to a hotel, the same one where Dennis and Dagmar are trying to be discreet. Oz's practical joke has Wayne and Barry scouring the corridors for their dates, and ruining Dennis's tête-à-tête in the process.

08: THE FUGITIVE

First broadcast: 6 January 1984

Oz is in a monumental sulk and refuses to go fishing with the other lads. On the trip they encounter a mysterious German stranger, Colin, played by Ray Winstone. It turns out he has gone AWOL from the British army after being bullied. As persuasive as ever, the lads convince him to return.

09: THE ALIEN

First broadcast: 13 January 1984

Bomber is absent for an episode and the spare bed in the hut is filled by the violent Irish nutcase McGowan. This disturbs the delicate equilibrium that had been created and even Oz seems perturbed by their new guest. They hatch a plan to get rid of him so that Bomber can have his bed back for Episode 10.

10: LAST RITES

First broadcast: 20 January 1984

Bomber is back, but he injures himself and requires hospital treatment. At the hospital Nev and Dennis befriend a miserable, dying Geordie who has lost touch with his family. When he dies Oz is very keen to transport his coffin back to England. He's not interested in the dearly departed, though; he wants to cram the coffin full of smuggled porn videos. The plan goes awry when the old man is cremated and Oz's business plan goes up in smoke.

11: THE LOVERS

First broadcast: 27 January 1984

Oz poses as a rich tycoon and falls in love with a German girl. When asked how his wife Marjorie will react to the affair he replies, 'We aren't exactly Charles and Diana.' (The two couples had more in common than he thought.) The German girl is not all she appears, however. She works at a sauna parlour. When her Turkish boyfriend finds out about Oz, he threatens him – but is persuaded not to carry out his threat by the lads, who convince him that Oz is 'otherwise inclined'. Barry painstakingly persuades the lads to redecorate the hut with paint lifted from the site.

12: LOVE AND OTHER FOUR LETTER WORDS

First broadcast: 3 February 1984

Vera is the latest wife to take the trip to Germany and tells Dennis, who is happily involved with Dagmar, that she wants him back. This puts our Den in a dilemma, but he is given little assistance by the rest of the lads. Wayne falls for the new secretary in the site office.

13: WHEN THE BOAT GOES OUT

First broadcast: 10 February 1984

The German government spoils everyone's fun by closing the tax loophole and forcing the lads into deciding whether to stay or go home. Dennis has to make up his mind between Düsseldorf and Newcastle, Dagmar and Vera, while the others wait to see what he does. Oz gets into a brawl, requires a blood transfusion and is pumped full of German blood – but is persuaded that Neville was the donor. Dennis spends one last night with Dagmar, but is interrupted when the lads arrive encrusted with soot because the hut has burned down.

SERIES TWO

PRINCIPAL CAST
Tim Healy: Dennis Patterson
Kevin Whately: Neville Hope
Jimmy Nail: Leonard 'Oz' Osbourne
Timothy Spall: Barry Taylor
Gary Holton: Wayne Norris
Pat Roach: 'Bomber' Busbridge
Chris Fairbank: Albert Arthur 'Moxey' Moxall

OTHER MAIN CAST
Julia Tobin: Brenda Hope
Bill Paterson: Ally Fraser
James Booth: Kenny Ames
Kevin Lloyd: Harry Blackburn
Su Elliott: Marjorie Osbourne
Madelaine Newton: Christine Chadwick
Val McLane: Norma Patterson
Lesley St John: Vicki
Bryan Pringle: Arthur Pringle
Melanie Hill: Hazel Redfern
John Bowler: Howard Radcliffe
Billy Geraghty: Paddy
Sammy Johnson: Martin Cooper
Simon Smith: Trevor
Morag Hood: Joy Chatterley
Catherine Rabett: Carol Pringle
Barry Hollinshead: Rod Osbourne
David Neville: Sir James Palmer
Ying Tong John: Big Baz
Victor Langley: Mr Treadaway
Paul Antony Barber: Russell, the camp tour-guide

01: THE RETURN OF THE SEVEN: PART ONE

First broadcast: 21 February 1986

Barry sends a letter to the lads, who are scattered across the country, asking for help to rebuild his house in time for his wedding to Hazel. One by one they show up: Bomber has been wrestling; Dennis has been drinking and falling in with a gangster; Neville has done little except fret; Wayne has returned from Germany, his marriage over; Moxey has been doing time, and Oz has been rebuilding the Falklands.

02: THE RETURN OF THE SEVEN: PART TWO

First broadcast: 28 February 1986

Dennis goes back to Newcastle and meets up with Oz, bringing him to Birmingham and so reuniting the seven once more. Once Barry's house is finished the lads are given another job: renovating Thornley Manor, a country house in the middle of nowhere. Barry's love life, meanwhile, verges towards the rocks.

03: A LAW FOR THE RICH

First Broadcast: 7 March 1986

Minus Barry, the gang arrive at Thornley Manor and the nearby village where the local landlord takes an immediate dislike to them. One of the locals reports the lads to the police, believing them to be housebreakers, which causes Moxey to make a bolt for it.

04: ANOTHER COUNTRY

First broadcast: 14 March 1986

It emerges that Thornley Manor is a listed building and the lads are forced to down tools. They are uncertain how to amuse themselves and Oz takes Barry trout tickling ending up in trouble with the local police. In the hotel bar there is class conflict when the locals take offence at the gang's uncouth manner, making Oz and Co. as 'welcome as a fart in an astronaut's suit'.

05: A HOME FROM HOME

First broadcast: 21 March 1986

Wayne's dalliance with Arthur the landlord's posh daughter gets the lads chucked out of the local hotel and they are forced to bunk down in a room in Thornley Manor. While investigating their new lodgings they come across a set of amateur videos, involving several local dignitaries in compromising positions. One of them turns out to be Arthur.

06: COWBOYS

First broadcast: 28 March 1986

A plumber who loves his country and western music turns up. He takes the lads to what must be the only country and western bar in the Midlands and we get to hear Oz sing a Merle Haggard song. The lads' noble refusal to cut corners on building an old people's home causes Ally Fraser to send his heavies in, resulting in an A-Team style fight in front of the house. The lads win.

07: NO SEX PLEASE, WE'RE BRICKIES

First broadcast: 4 April 1986

Fraser tempts the lads into completing their work on Thornley Manor with the promise of a new job in Spain. Arthur shops Wayne to customs and his car is impounded. In response the lads brick up the front door of the pub.

08: MARJORIE DOESN'T LIVE HERE ANYMORE

First broadcast: 11 April 1986

The lads wind up in Newcastle, while they wait for the job in Spain to come through,. Oz discovers that his wife plans to take his son to live in Italy with her new boyfriend. Stung into a rare fit of paternal feeling he endeavours to kidnap Rod, only for Wayne to hijack the wrong lad.

09: HASTA LA VISTA

First broadcast: 18 April 1986

Complications hold up the lads' journey to Spain, so they are forced to kick their heels in Newcastle for another episode. Moxey's latest disappearance looks like landing them with an extra builder no-one likes, until the Liverpool One makes another return. Finally, the lads are on their way to Spain, sharing a plane with the Spennymoor and District Senior Citizen Society.

10: SCOOP

First broadcast: 25 April 1986

In Spain at last, the gang make a splash when they are caught naked in a posh couple's swimming pool. A journalist mistakes them for a criminal gang and their arrival is splashed across a tabloid newspaper, sparking the interest of other hacks, and the admiration of an expatriate villain.

11: LAW AND DISORDER

First broadcast: 2 May 1986

Moxey falls in with local criminals at the English pub. Ally gives the lads a couple of days off to act like tourists and Barry and Moxey try, and fail, to make it to Gibraltar. Oz consoles them by describing it as 'like Filey with chimpanzees.' The lads are left with nothing else to do other than wander around town in horribly tight shorts trying to find entertainment.

12: FOR BETTER OR WORSE

First broadcast: 9 May 1986

Hazel shows up and Barry attempts to sort out the vexed question of their wedding. Meanwhile, the net closing in, and Ally tries to work a way of getting his money out of Britain and into Spain without going through customs. He suggests that Barry and Hazel get married on Kenny Ames's yacht so he can smuggle the cash via Tangiers.

13: QUO VADIS, PET

First broadcast: 16 May 1986

Barry chooses six best men; Oz woos Ally Fraser's girlfriend while Fraser's sorting out his affairs in Tangiers, then wins the Spanish lottery and buys the happy couple a big vase; and the pool is finished. Barry and Hazel get married on Kenny Ames's yacht and Ally meets the lads with a briefcase of cash, only for customs to intervene and chase the boat out to sea. The gang is last seen heading for Tangiers … 'There must be some work in North Africa,' opines Bomber. 'Oh there's bound to be,' says Moxey. 'They built the pyramids.'

SERIES THREE

PRINCIPAL CAST

Tim Healy: Dennis Patterson
Kevin Whately: Neville Hope
Jimmy Nail: Leonard 'Oz' Osbourne
Timothy Spall: Barry Taylor
Pat Roach: 'Bomber' Busbridge
Chris Fairbank: Albert Arthur 'Moxey' Moxall
Noel Clarke: Wyman

OTHER MAIN CAST

Julia Tobin: Brenda Hope
Bill Nighy: Jeffrey Grainger
Ron Donachie: Calhoun
Michael Angelis: Mickey Startup
Branka Katic: Tatiana Taylor
Emily Bruni: Sarah
Dragan Micanovic: Kadi
Joe Saugus: Gordon Tootoosis
Richard Ridings: DI Andy Hateley
Mark Stobbart: Rod Osbourne

01: BRIDGING THE GAP

First Broadcast: 28 April 2002

The lads reunite in Middlesbrough for Oz's funeral. Except he's not dead. Wayne is though, but his son Wyman turns up. Oz, fresh from prison, has befriended a crooked Tory and attempts to persuade his old mates who – apart from Barry who's now a fat millionaire – have fallen on hard times, to become involved in a scheme to take down the Transporter Bridge and sell it.

02: HEAVY METAL

First broadcast: 5 May 2002

The lads are now the gaffers, except they're in charge of a foreign work force – half Serb, half Kosovan – who become embroiled in internecine hatred. Meanwhile, it seems that Barry's business and his marriage to the voluptuous Tatiana are not all they appear to be.

03: BRIDGE OVER TROUBLED WATER

First broadcast: 12 May 2002

The deal to sell the bridge falls through. Startup sends his heavies in pursuit of Moxey and Barry becomes suspicious of Kadi. Oz goes with a few of the guys to watch his son sing Dusty Springfield covers – in drag, to his horror, giving us a glimpse of the old, intolerant Oz. However, he then shows how much he's changed, by scouring the Internet in search of a new buyer for the bridge.

04: A BRIDGE TOO FAR

First broadcast: 19 May 2002

A native American arrives in Middlesbrough with an intriguing offer: he wants the bridge. The seven's only problem is that they don't own it. Barry faces up to the truth about both his business and his marriage, while the lads, helpful as ever, rally round.

05: ANOTHER COUNTRY

First broadcast: 26 May 2002

The lads arrive in Arizona with the bridge. The only problem is that Kadi has smuggled drugs on to the plane, in revenge. Thrown out of their hotel when it is raided by gun-toting cops, they have nowhere to live. The solution? A hut, and a chance to relive old times. Wyman gets involved in trouble with the local rednecks and goes missing, while Oz walks across the Vegas skyline to ensure the bridge is finished. Dennis, still the gaffer, goes back to talk turkey with Grainger.

06: AN INSPECTOR CALLS

First broadcast: 2 June 2002

Vice, narcotics and rock music abound. Wyman is found because he was listening to Dire Straits rather than rap music; a cop arrives looking for Moxey, or so the lads think; Barry is interrogated over charges of drug smuggling; and Neville falls for the charms of a prostitute. Grainger turns up in Arizona, gets stoned and is arrested by DI Hateley. The job is finished and the lads leave – except for Bomber who is recovering from illness.